HIGHER CHOICES

HIGHER CHOICES

Life Enhancing Recipes

Second Edition

Janet Lasky

Foreword by Dr. Albrecht Heyer, Ph.D D.Sc. D.Ay. C.N.

Cover Drawing by Toni Chaplin

HIGHER CHOICES

Life Enhancing Recipes

By Janet Lasky

All rights reserved. No part of this publication may be reproduced in whole or in part in any form or by any means, electronic or mechanical, including photocopying, recording or by an information storage and retrieval system, without permission in writing by Janet Lasky.

Copyright © 1998 by Janet Lasky

First Edition 1998
Second Edition 1998

Library of Congress Catalogue Card Number: 98-92144

ISBN 0-9663603-1-1

Published by:
Higher Choices™ - Alternative Food Concepts, L.L.C.
Sparta, New Jersey

Printed in the United States of America

The information in this book is solely informational and not intended as medical advice in any given form, which may only be given by a qualified medical professional.

This book is dedicated to all those people who have come into my life to help me accept and embrace a healthier and happier way of eating.

CONTENTS

Foreword i
About the Author ii
Acknowledgments v
Introduction vi
An Efficient Kitchen 1
Menu 2
Shopping Guide for Food and Miscellaneous Products ... 3
Recommended Food & Miscellaneous Products 5
Eating Out 10
Ingredient Substitutes 11
Recipes 13
    Appetizers 14
    Soups 18
    Vegetables 25
    Salad Dressings, Sauces and Marinades 46
    Poultry 51
    Seafood 65
    Tofu 68
    Dried Beans & Lentils 72
    Grains 81
    Breads and Pancakes 82
    Perfect Snack 88
    Desserts 89
Index 106

Foreword

The role of nutrition in disease has been known since ancient times. Hippocrates said, "let thy food be thy medicine and let thy medicine be thy food." Unfortunately the role of food in human health is often overlooked and the average consumer is overwhelmed with substances that often have more additives than real nutrients. Sooner or later it will be discovered that the average diet with its high content of fat, carbohydrates, starches and additives is one of the leading contributors to many of the diseases we see today.

It is generally forgotten that for foods to fulfill their purpose in the body and mind they have to create harmony and biochemical balance. Unfortunately today's menus are more concerned with feeding addictions to food artifacts than to establish a state of harmony. Creating recipes which are free from what I consider disharmonious nutrients is no easy task. I want to commend Janet Lasky for undertaking the tedious work of designing and testing dishes which are not only very tasty, but also correspond to some of my recommendations for healthy and harmonious meals. The recipes presented in her book prove that good nutritious food does not have to be bland or dull. This book will make it easier for those who want a yeast, wheat, sugar, milk and ferment-free diet, to prepare exciting dishes without feeling deprived and discover the joy and benefits of healthy eating.

Albrecht A. Heyer, Ph.D. D.Sc. D.Ay. C.N.

About the Author

I grew up with poor eating habits, eating too many foods which contained sugar, fat and white flour products. There was an abundance of food in my home and I was encouraged to eat and enjoy the food my mother prepared. By the time I was six years old, I had developed a compulsive overeating disorder. I was grossly overweight most of my life. In my thirties, I developed high blood pressure, requiring the need for medication. Despite the fear of medical problems, I was unable to stick to any diet plan. Enjoying good tasting food and having an eating disorder was an almost deadly combination for me.

In 1989, my husband and I adopted a six year old boy. I realized this child needed a loving mother. It occurred to me that if I didn't get control of my eating, I would die an early death and deprive him of having a mother who truly loved him. I located an eating disorder program near my home and spent the next four years learning about my disorder, developing self-esteem and taking responsibility for my life. Shortly after I "graduated" from this program, I read Ruth Winter's book, called "Poisons in Your Food." It changed my outlook on the quality of the food produced in this country. Having evolved to a place where I wanted to be as healthy as possible, I began investigating organic foods. I learned where to find health food stores, cooperatives, restaurants and related services. I was excited about all this new information, but I wanted to refine my daily routine even more.

In 1994, I was fortunate to meet Dr. A. Heyer, a certified nutritionist, based in New York City. Along with a lot of valuable advice, information and a list of organic foods to eat, he suggested that I eliminate wheat, sugar, yeast, milk and fermented products from my diet. I went home with all this new information, filled with hope and excitement. Those happy feelings soon turned into confusion and doubt. How was I going to make meals which my family and I could enjoy? If I chose to follow Dr. Heyer's advice, what was I going to eat for breakfast the next day? The answers to those questions did not come quickly or easily. Within the first few weeks of trying to follow this new way of eating, I felt lost, alone and very hungry. I wasn't eating very much because I felt disoriented and unsure of all the foods available for me to eat and how to actually prepare the food. I had been a very good cook, yet suddenly I felt unable to prepare the simplest recipe.

With the help of many people, I learned how to rethink my way of cooking and eating. I began to try foods that I had never eaten before. I also discovered healthier substitutes for the ingredients I no longer eat. By using these substitutes, I could use my old recipes or most cookbook recipes to make a healthy meal. I continue to experiment and try new ideas all the time. Today, my family and I enjoy wonderfully prepared foods. By using your time efficiently and wisely, you too can create healthier versions of the recipes you have been using and enjoying.

In the four years since changing my eating habits numerous and wonderful physical changes have occurred. I have lost 130 pounds. I no longer require blood pressure medication, because my blood pressure is always within normal limits. Despite the fact that I was diagnosed with diabetes four years ago, my blood sugar levels are always within normal range and my cholesterol has dropped from 200 to 144. I feel great and I rarely experience any physical discomfort or illness.

My commitment to choosing foods which are right for me is an important element in the good health I enjoy today. I eat mainly vegetables, proteins, beans, lentils, fruit and soy cheese products. I rarely eat certain carbohydrates (pasta, breads, cakes) and grains (rice and oatmeal), since I tend to gain weight. I snack on dry roasted sunflower seeds. I take vitamins, minerals and supplements which enhance my food plan. I also maintain a regular exercise program which includes aerobic work outs and weight lifting. I drink water that has been purified by a reverse osmosis filter system and decaffeinated herbal tea. I am not on a diet and so, this is not a diet book. I offer this as an alternative way to work with food. I do not count calories and I do not have to worry about my fat intake, since I use only butter, grape seed, canola or olive oil and soy cheese products in very small amounts.

I wrote this book because I thought it would help Dr. Heyer's clients as they changed their eating habits. Soon after the book became available to the public, I realized that people with food and chemical allergies, medical problems and people wanting to make healthier food choices were eager to learn about alternative ways of cooking. I invite you to try my style of cooking. I wish you good luck and good health.

If you have any questions or comments, please contact me by regular mail or e-mail.

Janet Lasky
October 1998

Photo by Robin Schwartz

Acknowledgments

I would like to thank Larry Lasky for encouraging me to write this book.

I would like to thank Dr. Heyer for his knowledge and patience. I would like to thank Aurora Mayet for opening many doors for me. She introduced me to Dr. Heyer and she continues to encourage and support me in many ways. I would like to thank Toni Chaplin for her patience, ideas and artistic ability in designing the book cover. I am grateful to Irene Linck for her editing skills, patience and support. I would like to thank my son Paul for coming into my life and changing it forever.

Introduction

The purpose of this book is twofold: to serve as a guide to finding the highest quality food available and to work with healthy food substitutes, so that you can make interesting and satisfying meals.

The recipes included in this book are either my own creations or old recipes which I have adapted to my new way of cooking. Do not hesitate to go through your recipes and cookbooks and make the necessary changes needed to follow your new food plan. Just make your substitutions and have fun. Use organic products whenever possible. Use fresh food as much as possible. Experiment with foods and herbs you have never tried before. Also, remember that the amounts of butter, oil and seasonings can be adapted to suit your tastes and food plan constraints, so use more or less of the seasonings as you prefer. Do not be afraid to make something, even though you do not have a substitute ingredient for a particular item. For your convenience, I have included a list of ingredient substitutes on pages 11-12. Try the substitutions. I think you will be happy with the way they maintain the integrity of a recipe.

Because I cook everything from scratch, it takes time to prepare healthy meals. No hamburger helper in this kitchen. However, there are "short cuts" to save time. Use a crock pot to cook meals while you are at work. Use a pressure cooker to shorten the cooking time of such items as beans and vegetables. Cook large portions of food and freeze them. If you have a busy life style like I do, you will do whatever you can to make cooking quicker and easier.

Shopping guide for food and miscellaneous products

Initially, I spent many hours searching for sources of organic and high quality non-organic food. Check your telephone book or call your local, county or state offices for information regarding the locations of organic farms, health food stores, organic food co-operatives, organic restaurants and pharmacies which carry vitamins, supplements, herbal tea, homeopathic medicine, personal hygiene products and books. You can also look for a local chapter of your state's organic farming association for information. The Organic Trade Association, a national trade alliance, can help you in your search. Call 413-774-7511 or visit www.ota.com. In your travels, talk to as many people as you can. I have often struck up a conversation with a fellow consumer in a health food store and have learned valuable information. If you own a computer, use the Internet to gather information.

I buy my seafood from Katch Seafoods in Homer, Alaska (800-368-7400). They have a wonderful selection of salmon, shrimp, halibut, scallops and king crab legs. Their fish is caught in Kachemak Bay, vacuum packed and frozen in meal size packages. They ship anywhere in the United States and will send the order to your home or office, guaranteeing one day delivery. Although there is a shipping charge for this service, the total cost of the fish and the shipping is similar in price to what I pay for fish per pound in my local seafood store and sometimes it is even cheaper.

There is a free pamphlet available for New Jersey, New York, Long Island, Connecticut, and the San Francisco Bay area. For New Jersey, it is called, "New Jersey Naturally, The Community Directory for Natural Living." New York, Long Island, Connecticut and San Francisco Bay area are listed the same way. This pamphlet lists a calendar of events, a natural living marketplace, natural food restaurants and a take-out and deli guide. The pamphlets also include discount coupons. So, when you need a break from cooking, treat yourself and go out to a restaurant which prepares organic food. You can call 800-486-4794 for more information. Although these particular pamphlets are not yet available in all areas of the country, you may find something similar in your state.

Recommended food and miscellaneous products

Bread, Bread Products, Cookies, Cereal, Pasta

French Meadow Bakery – Organic bread products free of wheat, yeast, sweeteners, oil and dairy

Ener G Wheat and Yeast Free White Rice Loaf

Nature's Warehouse - Wheat free, fruit juice sweetened pastry poppers

Pamela's Cookies - Some are wheat free and sweetened with fruit juice

Cereals - Go by the ingredients and what you like

Rice Pasta - I've tried at least 3-4 brands - all similar, all good

Spelt Pasta - Vita Spelt

Fearn Rice Baking Mix - It is wheat and gluten free. I use it for pancakes and waffles. I also use it to bread chicken and fish.

Edward and Sons Brown Rice Snaps (crackers) - Use only the crackers that are free of fermented products

Lundberg Organic Brown Rice Cakes - Salt Free

Recommended food and miscellaneous products

Canned Foods

Muir Glen Organic Tomato Products - Crushed, whole, purée, tomato sauce, tomato paste, etc.

Eden - Organic beans - all varieties

Westbrae - Organic beans - all varieties

Bearitos Organic Refried Beans

Solana Gold Organic Applesauce - Use flavors without added sugar

Ceres Fruit Juices — 100% pure fruit juice

Lakewood Organic Pineapple Juice - 100% pure fruit juice

Sir Real Organic Apple Butter and Applesauce (Original and Golden Delicious) - Unsweetened

Harvest Moon and Crofters Organic Fruit Spreads - Sweetened with fruit juice

Cascadian Farms Organic Fruit Conserves - Sweetened with fruit juice

Natural Sea Tuna

Pacific Foods of Oregon Free-Range Chicken or Organic Vegetable Broth

Recommended food and miscellaneous products

Frozen Foods

Cascadian Farms - Organic vegetables, fruit and sorbet

Sno-Pac - Organic vegetables

Organic Valley Sweet Butter

Earth Sky Protein Burgers (vegetable patties)

Van's Wheat-Free Waffles

Flour for baking bread products

I use Arrowhead Mills Organic Flour. Use oat, spelt, brown rice, and barley flour as substitutes for wheat flour. I find that spelt flour has the best flavor. I use it for my pie crusts and biscuits. Barley flour has a strong flavor, so I mix it with brown rice flour. Oat flour is good for biscuits and pancakes. For cookies and cakes, I use 3/4 cup oat flour and 1/4 cup barley flour or 3/4 cup brown rice flour and 1/4 cup barley flour instead of 1 cup of regular flour. Oat flour tends to be lumpy, so I sift it twice. You can buy 2 pound bags or save money and buy flour in bulk (5 lbs.), depending on how much you plan to use. I freeze all my flour (for that matter, I freeze any rice and other grains for about 5-7 days to kill any bugs that might be in the bag.) Then, I store everything in my refrigerator in airtight containers.

Recommended food and miscellaneous products

Grains

I think I've tried them all. There is barley, buckwheat, millet, oats, quinoa, basmati rice (the best rice I have ever tasted), brown rice, spelt berries, rye berries and wild rice. Try them all and find the ones you like.

Miscellaneous Food Products

Westbrae Natural - Westsoy organic unsweetened non-dairy soy beverage

Edensoy Milk - Extra Regular and Vanilla, Eden Blend Rice and Soy Milk

Enriched Rice Dream (rice milk) - Plain and vanilla

Fresh Tofu Inc. - Organic tofu

Soya Kaas Soy Cheese Products

Lite and Less Grated Parmesan Cheese Alternative

Spectrum Organic Canola and Olive Oil

California Naturals Organic Grape Seed Oil

Bragg Liquid Aminos - All purpose seasoning

Arrowhead Mills Organic Sesame Tahini

Frontier Organic Non-Irradiated Seasonings

Frontier Organic Extracts and Flavors

Recommended food and miscellaneous products

Miscellaneous Food Products

Featherweight Baking Powder

Lima Sea Salt

NOW FOODS - Stevia powder (a natural sweetener)

NOW FOODS - Carob drops - Unsweetened and dairy free

Shiloh Farms – Coconut - Unsweetened and unsulphured

Miscellaneous Non-Food Products

Dynamo 2 - For cleaning raw fruits and vegetables and to use in drinking water

Kiss My Face Skin and Hair Products

E-Cover Laundry Detergent

Ecco Bella and Aveda Cosmetics

Natracare - All cotton feminine products

Homeodent 2 - Natural toothpaste

I try to use organic and natural products as much as possible.

NOTE: Most health food stores will give you a 10% discount if you order by the case.

Eating out

We do not go out very often anymore and that is by choice. If we do go out, we select a restaurant that serves organically prepared food, or a better quality restaurant and order fish, lamb or vegetables which are plain grilled or broiled. I also use a local Chinese take-out and request my selection steamed (crispy). When I get it home, I put the food in my frying pan and add 1-2 teaspoons of Bragg Liquid Aminos, fresh garlic or garlic powder, sea salt and pepper. I cook the vegetables until they are well heated and lightly browned. It's delicious! Moo Shu works very well. Chinese cooking is perfect for our way of eating, it just may take a little time to convince the Chinese chefs to prepare it your way. Our chef laughs and says "No Taste."

A good Italian restaurant will have fresh fish selections and they will have a lot of vegetables from which to choose. Order steamed vegetables such as escarole, spinach, mushrooms, broccoli and peppers and ask for a little marinara sauce on the side.

Ingredient Substitutes

The following list of ingredient substitutes forms the foundation of my way of cooking. I have found that these products are wonderful replacements for the foods I no longer eat. I am able to create healthy and delicious recipes. I never feel deprived that I no longer eat wheat, sugar, yeast, milk or fermented products. The only difference I detect is in my dessert recipes. They are not sugary sweet yet, they still have a delicious flavor and consistency. If you choose not to eat sugar, you will be glad to have these alternative recipes.

- Fresh lemon or lime juice replaces vinegar
- Bragg Liquid Aminos replaces soy sauce
- Soymilk or rice milk replaces animal milk
- Spelt, oat, brown rice, barley and other alternative flours replace wheat flour
- Stevia powder (a natural sweetener), unsweetened applesauce, unsweetened apple butter, vanilla extract, and jams sweetened with fruit juice only replace sugar and honey
- Dry chili pepper flakes, cumin, garlic powder, oregano, coriander, allspice, cloves, salt, pepper, paprika, pinch of cayenne, turmeric, lots of crushed fresh garlic, and a little lemon juice replace taco seasoning
- Soy products such as tofu and soy cheese replace mozzarella cheese, ricotta cheese and sour cream (rice cheese is available also)
- Sea Salt replaces regular salt

Cont'd

Ingredient Substitutes

- Dry mustard mixed with a little water, oil, tarragon, salt, pepper, garlic powder, ground celery seed or root, thyme, onion powder and any other spices you like, makes a good substitute for prepared mustard. Add water a little at a time until desired consistency is achieved.
- Unsweetened and dairy free carob chips replace chocolate chips
- Unsweetened, dairy free roasted carob powder replaces cocoa powder

Recipes

I am not a professionally trained chef. Most of the recipes included in this book are my own creation or an adaptation of other recipes. Try the recipes as they are written and then adjust them to your own taste.

The most common methods of cooking which I use are steaming, broiling, roasting, baking and grilling. Although I am allowed to use butter and oil, I use them sparingly. I recommend using grape seed oil. It withstands heat better than any other oil. I also use canola and olive oil in some recipes. I no longer sauté garlic, onions, or any food in fat because it is not a healthy way of cooking. Choose from one of the following methods to replace using fat in a sauté pan:

> Use water or broth in a sauté pan to cook garlic or other vegetables. If you want the flavor of olive oil, add the oil to the vegetables after they have been removed from the pan. Another method is to put any food such as garlic, herbs, onions, peppers, etc. into an oven proof dish. Add about 1 tablespoon of grape seed oil and cook the vegetables or herbs in a 300° oven until soft, but not brown.

Before I use raw vegetables or fruits, I soak them in a mixture of purified water and 10-12 drops of Dynamo 2 to help eliminate bacteria.

Use organic products as much as possible. Check ingredients to be sure the item is free of wheat, sugar, yeast, milk and fermented products. Food products in health food stores are free of chemicals and preservatives, but many items have sugar, yeast, etc. Choose wisely and carefully. Try to avoid using food from cans. Use fresh produce, beans, etc. as much as possible.

Appetizers

The following appetizers are easy to prepare and delicious. I make them for guests and I take them with me when I go to a party at someone else's home. Enjoy!

Black Bean Hummus

- 2 cups garbanzo beans, cooked (**see page** 72) or 1 can, rinsed and drained
- 2 cups black beans, cooked (**see page** 72) or 1 can, rinsed and drained
- ¼ cup sesame tahini
- 2 tablespoons olive or canola oil
- 2 cloves garlic, or more to taste, chopped
- ½ teaspoon Bragg Liquid Aminos
- ¼-½ of a lemon - juice only
- ½-1 teaspoon sea salt to taste
- freshly ground pepper to taste
- ½ bar firm tofu - broken up into small pieces (optional)

Put all the ingredients into a food processor and blend until creamy. Serve as a dip with vegetables, rice crackers or spelt bread. To make red pepper hummus, omit the black beans and use a small red pepper (remove the seeds and chop). Put the pepper into the food processor along with the other ingredients and blend. Make the red pepper hummus 24 hours before serving.

Lentil Pate'

- 2 cups lentils, cooked **(see page 72)** or 1 can, rinsed and drained
- 1 small onion, finely chopped
- 1 tablespoon grape seed oil
- 2 tablespoons canola oil
- 1 teaspoon Bragg Liquid Aminos
- 1 hard boiled egg (optional)
- 1 teaspoon sea salt
- freshly ground pepper to taste

Preheat oven to 350°. Put ½ of the chopped onion in a small oven proof dish. Add 1 tablespoon of grape seed oil and 1 teaspoon of Bragg Liquid Aminos to the onions. Put the onions into the oven and cook for about 15 minutes or until soft and slightly browned. Rinse and drain the lentils and put them into a food processor. Add the raw onion, the cooked onion, 2 tablespoons of canola oil, the hard boiled egg, sea salt and freshly ground pepper. Blend until creamy. Add more oil if you want the mixture to be creamier. Adjust sea salt and pepper to your taste. Serve with celery sticks or rice crackers.

Onion Dip

- 1 container of Soya Kaas plain "Cream Cheese"
- 4 ounces plain soy or rice milk
- 3 tablespoons onion flakes
- 3 teaspoons dried, chopped chives
- 1 teaspoon garlic powder
- 1 teaspoon browned onion granules
- 1 teaspoon soy "Parmesan Cheese"
- ½ teaspoon onion powder
- ¼ - ½ teaspoon sea salt
- ⅛ teaspoon freshly ground pepper

Put the "cream cheese" into a small mixing bowl. Stir with a spoon until it is creamy. Add the milk and blend, using a spoon or whisk. The mixture should have the consistency of sour cream, so add more soy or rice milk if necessary. Add all the other ingredients and mix well. Adjust seasonings to your taste. Chill before serving. This recipe is very versatile. It is a delicious dip and if you add more soy or rice milk, you can create a salad dressing, mayonnaise or a marinade for chicken and fish.

Tofu Dip

- 1 package of soft tofu
- 2 tablespoons canola oil
- 1 teaspoon lemon juice
- ½ teaspoon garlic powder
- ¼ teaspoon freshly ground pepper
- ⅓ teaspoon Bragg Liquid Aminos
- 1 clove of garlic, minced
- ½ cup of fresh chopped chives or use dried chives to taste
- onion flakes, onion powder, parsley, to taste
- plain soy or rice milk (use to thin out the tofu)

Drain the tofu and then break it up and put it into a food processor. Add all the other ingredients except the milk. Process until creamy. Add milk to achieve the desired consistency of sour cream. Adjust seasonings to your taste. Chill before serving.

Soups

Most of the soup you now make will easily adapt to your new style of cooking. Look at the ingredients and just omit whatever ingredients you no longer use. Here are a few of my favorite soup recipes.

Lentil Soup

- 2 cups uncooked lentils
- 10 cups water
- 1 onion, chopped
- 2 leeks, chopped, rinsed and drained (use the whole leek)
- 4 carrots, chopped
- 2 celery stalks, chopped
- 2 medium white potatoes, chopped
- 1 package of mushrooms, cleaned and sliced
- 1 cup or more of collard greens, chopped
- 1-2 teaspoons sea salt
- 2 bay leaves
- 2 cloves garlic, crushed
- ¼ teaspoon thyme
- 1 teaspoon Bragg Liquid Aminos
- ¼ cup pearl barley (optional)
- freshly ground pepper to taste

Wash and drain the lentils. Put lentils, water and sea salt in pot and bring to a boil. Add onion, leeks, carrots, celery, potatoes, mushrooms, collard greens and seasonings. Cover, reduce heat and simmer 1½ hours or until vegetables are tender.

Note: To make this more like a stew, use 7 cups of water. I have also added a little mild curry to this dish, which gives it an interesting flavor.

Minestrone

- 8-10 cups water
- ½ cup kidney beans, cooked **(see page 72)** or ½ can, rinsed and drained
- ¼ cup onion, chopped
- 1 leek, chopped
- 1 clove garlic, crushed
- 2 or more cups shredded cabbage
- 1 small turnip, peeled and diced
- 1 cup carrots, sliced
- 1 cup zucchini, diced
- 1 cup celery, chopped
- ½ cup frozen peas
- 1 teaspoon parsley, chopped (fresh or dry)
- 1 teaspoon chopped basil
- ¼ teaspoon oregano
- 1 cup spinach, collard greens or any other leafy green vegetable
- 1 can (14½ oz.) whole peeled tomatoes
- 1 can (6 oz.) tomato paste
- ½ cup wheat-free pasta (optional)
- 1 teaspoon sea salt
- ¼ teaspoon freshly ground pepper

Put ¼ cup of water into a large soup pot and heat. Add onion and cook for a few minutes and then add the leek and cabbage and cook until soft. Add 8 cups of water and bring to a boil. Add all ingredients except the beans, peas and pasta and cook 30 minutes. Add beans, peas and pasta and simmer 10 minutes more.

Mushroom Barley Soup

- ¾ cup raw pearl barley
- 1 large onion, chopped
- 2 celery stalks, finely chopped
- 1 large carrot, sliced
- 2 bay leaves
- 2 tablespoons butter
- 6 cups chicken broth, vegetable stock or water
- ¼ teaspoon dried dill
- ½ teaspoon dried summer savory
- 10-12 ounces white mushrooms, coarsely chopped
- 2 cups plain soy or rice milk (more or less as needed)
- sea salt and freshly ground pepper to taste

Place the barley, onion, celery, carrot, bay leaves and butter in a large soup pot with vegetable stock or water and seasonings. Bring to a boil, cover and simmer over moderate low heat for 30 minutes. Add the mushrooms and simmer another 20 minutes, or until the vegetables are tender. Stir in enough soy or rice milk to get a slightly thick consistency. Allow the soup to stand for 30 minutes off the heat before serving. The soup thickens quite a bit if it is refrigerated. Add more milk or stock as needed and adjust seasonings.

Split Pea Soup

- 2 cups uncooked split peas, rinsed and drained
- 8 cups water
- 2 small potatoes (white or sweet)
- 2 celery stalks, chopped
- 2 carrots, sliced
- 2 leeks or 1 large onion, chopped
- 1 clove garlic, crushed
- 1 bay leaf
- ½ teaspoon thyme
- 1-2 teaspoons sea salt
- 1 teaspoon garlic powder
- 1 teaspoon Bragg Liquid Aminos
- freshly ground pepper to taste

Put water and peas into a large pot. Bring to a boil and simmer slowly for 2-3 hours. Stir occasionally. Add all vegetables and seasonings and cook for 45 minutes to 1 hour longer. I take the vegetables out of the soup and pour the liquid into a food processor and blend to thicken it. Put the vegetables back into the soup and stir the mixture. This soup freezes well.

Myra's Chicken Soup

My mother makes the best chicken soup in the world. Now you can too!

1	Pullet (3-4 lbs.)	1	teaspoon fresh dill
4	carrots, chopped	¼	cup fresh parsley
2	celery stalks, chopped	1	teaspoon garlic powder
2	medium onions, chopped		sea salt and freshly ground pepper to taste
1	parsnip, cut into pieces		
1	turnip, cut into pieces		
2	leeks, chopped, rinsed and drained		

Put chicken into cold water to cover it. Add sea salt, pepper and garlic powder. Bring to a boil. Skim the foam from the surface of the water. After the foam stops forming, add all the vegetables and seasonings. Simmer for 1 hour. Take the chicken out and remove the meat from the bones. Put the chicken back into the pot. This soup freezes well.

Vegetable Bean Soup

- 8 cups of water
- 1 medium onion, chopped
- 1 large leek, chopped
- 3-4 carrots, sliced
- 1-2 cloves garlic, chopped
- 1-2 celery stalks, chopped
- 1 yellow squash, chopped
- 1 parsnip, chopped
- 1 turnip, chopped
- ½ cup collard greens or spinach, chopped
- 1 bay leaf
- 1 8 ounce can of plain tomato sauce
- 1 teaspoon sea salt
- 1 teaspoon garlic powder
- ⅛ teaspoon oregano
- 2 cups kidney beans, cooked **(see page 72)** or 1 can, rinsed and drained
- 2 cups great northern beans, cooked **(see page 72)** or 1 can, rinsed and drained
- freshly ground pepper to taste

Put all ingredients except the beans into a pot. Bring the mixture to a boil and simmer for about 45 minutes to an hour, or until the vegetables are tender. Adjust your seasonings, add beans and cook a few minutes more.

Vegetable Soup

- 3 carrots, diced
- 1 large onion, diced
- 2 leeks, washed and sliced
- 2 celery stalks, diced
- 6 cups water or stock, heated
- 1 large can of tomato sauce, chunky tomatoes or tomato purée
- 2 small potatoes, diced
- ½ small turnip, diced
- 2 tablespoons parsley, chopped
- 1 teaspoon sea salt
- ½ teaspoon pepper
- ⅛ teaspoon oregano or to taste
- 1 cup chopped cabbage
- 1 cup collard greens
- ½ cup peas
- 2 cups kidney beans, cooked **(see page 72)** or 1 can, rinsed and drained
- 1 zucchini, chopped
- ½ cup frozen or fresh string beans
- ½ cup pearl barley, optional
- ½ cup wheat-free pasta, optional

Put water or stock into a small sauté pan and heat. Add carrots, onion, leek and celery and sauté briefly. In a large soup pot, heat water and add tomatoes, potatoes, turnip, string beans, collard greens, sea salt, pepper, parsley, oregano, pasta and barley. Cook covered about 35 minutes and then add cabbage, peas, kidney beans and zucchini. Cook about 10 minutes more. For a different texture, blend the soup in a food processor to create a vegetable purée.

VEGETABLES

If you are on a rotation food plan, the more vegetables you are willing to eat the more variety you will have. I have been eating vegetables that I had never even heard of until recently. Experiment and have fun. Leafy green vegetables like spinach, escarole, Swiss chard, etc. are delicious sautéed with broth and fresh garlic. Root vegetables like sweet potatoes, turnips, parsnips and rutabaga make a wonderful roasted casserole when mixed with some oil and herbs. Grill, sauté (with water or soup stock only), stir-fry, roast, steam, bake, boil and broil vegetables. Try different herbs to vary the flavor.

Try washing and cutting up various vegetables (leek, peppers, collard greens, and spinach). Put them into self-sealing plastic bags and freeze them. Add them to stews, chili and soups. When cooking fresh beets, peel them immediately after cooking. The skins slide off easily when the beets are warm.

When you clean your vegetables, use a small plastic bucket or container. Fill it with water and leave it in your sink. Put vegetables into the bucket of water, add Dynamo 2 and clean them. This saves on water and it is a very easy way to clean any vegetable.

Stir Fry

Before stir frying vegetables, throw the cut up pieces into boiling water for 1-2 minutes and then drain them. Slice or mince garlic and put it into a small oven dish. Add about 1 tablespoon of grape seed oil and bake the garlic for about 20 minutes in a 300° oven or until it is soft. Watch the garlic and stir occasionally to avoid burning it. Throw the vegetables into a large frying pan, add a little water or broth, a little Bragg Liquid Aminos, sea salt and pepper. You can cook so many vegetables this way. Cut them into different shapes and sizes. Broccoli, carrots, cabbage, peppers, onions, pea pods, mushrooms, bok choy, celery, zucchini and eggplant are just a few of the vegetables you can stir fry. Cook the vegetables quickly and add the garlic when you are done stir frying.

Roasted Vegetables

Set oven to 450°. Take a large self-sealing plastic bag and put 1-2 tablespoons of grape seed oil into the bag. Generously shake in pepper, garlic and onion powder, paprika and parsley. Use about 1 teaspoon of sea salt. Add any vegetables that you will be using for that meal. Use at least 1-2 lbs. of mixed vegetables. Seal the bag and shake until vegetables are well coated. Open the bag and pour the vegetables into a large roasting pan. Throw the plastic bag away. Roast vegetables, stirring occasionally until tender, about 30-40 minutes. Carrots, white potatoes, onions, peppers, eggplant and zucchini are delicious. Firmer vegetables take longer to cook, so put them in first. Figure 40 minutes for potatoes, 25 minutes for carrots, onions, peppers and eggplant, and 20 minutes for zucchini.

Grilled Vegetables

I usually slice up my vegetables and then lightly brush them with a little grape seed oil. Then I sprinkle garlic powder, sea salt and pepper on them and put them under the broiler or on the outdoor grill.

Sautéed Vegetables

Avoid using oil or butter to sauté vegetables. Use the following directions to replace your usual method of sautéing. I love escarole, spinach and Swiss chard sautéed with garlic. Use 1 to 2 lbs. of greens. Rinse the greens first. Chop up lots of fresh garlic. Put garlic into a small ovenproof dish, add 1 tablespoon of grape seed oil and bake at 300° for about 20 minutes. Watch the garlic and stir occasionally until soft. Heat a large frying pan (medium high), put the slightly wet greens into the pan, add ¼ cup of water or broth and cover the pan. When you see steam coming out from under the lid, turn the temperature down to a simmer and cook about 5 minutes. Transfer the greens to a serving bowl and add the cooked garlic. Season with sea salt and pepper to taste. If you want to, you can now add a little olive oil or butter to this dish. Try using different greens at the same time.

Avocado Salad

- 1 ripe avocado cut in half, scoop out meat and mash with a fork
- 1 hard boiled egg, mashed (optional)
- 1 tomato, finely diced (optional)
- ½ medium onion, finely diced
- 1 teaspoon of fresh lemon juice or more to taste
- sea salt to taste

Combine all ingredients in a bowl. Put avocado pit into the bowl to prevent browning and chill before serving. If you won't be using the salad right away, don't add the chopped tomatoes until you are ready to serve the salad. This recipe can be used as an appetizer too!

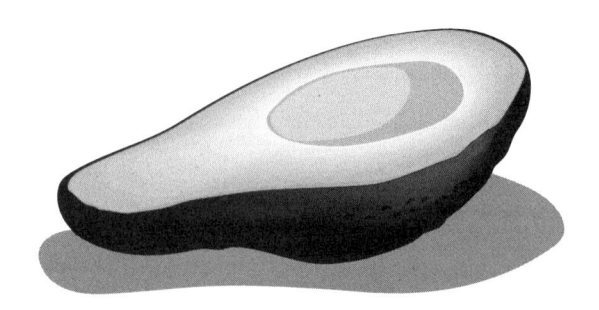

Green Bean Casserole

Remember the green bean casserole made with Cream of Mushroom Soup and canned onion rings? Well, I've recreated it using healthier ingredients.

2 lbs. fresh green beans, cut french style (cut beans in half, lengthwise)	1 recipe of basic white sauce (page 47)
1 lb. fresh mushrooms, cleaned and sliced or chopped	2 tablespoons onion flakes, lightly toasted
	sea salt and freshly ground pepper to taste

Preheat oven to 350°. Steam sliced beans for 4-5 minutes. Make white sauce. Mix beans, mushrooms, white sauce and seasonings and pour into a baking dish. Bake for about 20-30 minutes.

Stir Fried Green Beans

3-4 cloves garlic, thinly sliced
1 lb. fresh green beans or pole beans, rinsed and drained
1 tablespoon grape seed oil
sea salt and freshly ground pepper to taste
water

Fill a large skillet or wok about halfway with water. Bring to a boil. Steam the green beans for about 4-5 minutes, depending upon how crispy you like them. Put the garlic and grape seed oil into an oven dish and bake it in a 300° oven until soft. Stir the garlic often to prevent it from burning. Remove the garlic and set it aside. Drain the beans. Put beans back into the large skillet and sauté them over high heat for a couple of minutes, until the beans start to brown. Put beans into a serving dish and mix with the garlic and oil. Season the beans with sea salt and pepper to taste.

Broiled Broccoli with Garlic

1   bunch of broccoli
3-4 cloves of garlic,
    thinly sliced
water

1   tablespoon grape seed oil
    fresh lemon juice
sea salt and freshly ground
    pepper to taste

Cut up broccoli, wash and drain. Steam for 1-2 minutes and drain. Bake garlic in 1 tablespoon of grape seed oil in a 300° oven. Watch garlic and stir often to prevent it from burning. Place broccoli and garlic into a broiling pan. Squeeze a small piece of lemon over the vegetables. Add sea salt and pepper to taste and toss. Place under broiler and watch carefully as it begins to brown. Stir and cook for about 10 minutes. Heat a can of organic Cannelloni beans and mix with the broccoli and garlic for a delicious meal.

Grandma Rose's Roasted Carrots

My maternal grandmother was a wonderful cook. I think of her when I make these carrots because the seasonings remind me of a dish she used to make.

- 2 lbs. carrots, scrubbed, washed and cut up in any size or shape you desire
- 2 leeks, chopped and washed (optional) or dried chives to taste
- garlic powder, onion powder, parsley, paprika to taste
- ½ teaspoon sea salt and freshly ground pepper to taste
- grape seed oil

Preheat oven to 425°. Put about 2 tablespoons of oil into a large roasting pan. Add seasonings and stir. Throw in carrots and mix until coated. Place pan in oven and roast for about 45 minutes, stirring every 10-15 minutes or so. The dish my grandmother used to make included chicken and potatoes as well as the carrots. Try it, I'm sure you will like it.

Eggplant Parmigiana

2 medium sized eggplants, cleaned and cut lengthwise into ¼" slices
marinara sauce (page 47)
grape seed oil

1 package Soya Kaas "Mozzarella Cheese," shredded
2 tablespoons grated Soy "Parmesan Cheese"

Preheat oven to 425°. Lightly brush both sides of the eggplant slices with oil. Arrange on a shallow oven dish and bake for 10 minutes, then turn over and continue baking for another 8-10 minutes until the eggplant is soft and lightly browned. Remove the eggplant from the oven. Use a fairly deep baking dish to arrange the ingredients. Put sauce in first, then a layer of eggplant, mozzarella cheese, and Parmesan cheese. Repeat layers until you use up all the ingredients, saving some cheese for the top. Turn down the oven to 350° and bake for about 20 minutes or until the cheese has melted and is slightly browned.

Roasted Eggplant and Garbanzo Beans

- 1 medium eggplant, cut into cubes (with or without skin)
- 2 cups garbanzo beans, cooked **(see page 72)** or 1 can, rinsed and drained
- 1 medium red or yellow pepper, cut into chunks (optional)
- 1 medium onion, cut into chunks
- 1 clove garlic, finely chopped
- 3 tablespoons grape seed oil, or more if needed
- 3 tablespoons plain tomato sauce (optional)
- 1 teaspoon ground cumin, or more to taste
- sea salt and freshly ground pepper to taste

Preheat oven to 350°. Put the eggplant, garbanzo beans, pepper, onion, garlic, oil, tomato sauce, cumin, salt and freshly ground pepper into a large self-sealing plastic bag. Shake until vegetables are well coated. Put all the ingredients into a baking dish and throw the bag away. If you do not have plastic bags, put all the ingredients into the baking pan and mix until well coated. Bake 45 minutes or until the eggplant is soft and the onions are brown. While the vegetables are baking, stir them occasionally and add additional oil if you feel the mixture is too dry. If you do not want to use more oil, use the tomato sauce to moisten the vegetables. Adjust the seasonings and serve warm or room temperature. This is a wonderful main entrée or side dish.

Oven "Fried" Sweet Onions

If you like fried onions, you will love this recipe!

2 large sweet onions
1 tablespoon grape seed oil
1 tablespoon Bragg Liquid Aminos or water

Preheat oven to 450°. Peel onions and slice into rings. Combine onions with remaining ingredients in a large self-sealing plastic bag. Close bag tightly and shake to coat. Pour onions into a shallow baking dish and throw away the bag. Place pan on bottom shelf of oven and bake until done - about 30 minutes. You can also cook these onions on the grill.

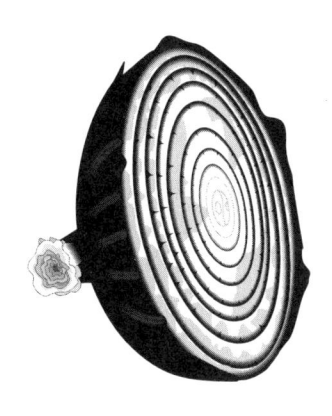

Denise's Potato Salad

This is the best potato salad I have ever eaten and it is free of mayonnaise and sugar!

- 5 lbs red or white potatoes -boiled whole and then cut up
- 2 celery stalks, chopped
- 1 red onion, sliced
- 1 can black olives
- 6 fresh basil leaves, thinly sliced
- ¼ - ½ cup of olive oil
- juice from one lemon
- 1 teaspoon sea salt (or more to taste)
- freshly ground pepper to taste

Boil the potatoes until you can pierce them with a knife or fork. Take the potatoes out of the water and put them into a colander. Put the oil, lemon juice, salt and freshly ground pepper into a large mixing bowl. Using a whisk, beat the ingredients until well blended. Cut the potatoes up into chunks or slices. You can leave the potato skins on or take them off. Put the potatoes, celery, onion, olives, and basil into the lemon/oil mixture and gently mix. This salad can be eaten warm or chilled. You can add your favorite vegetables to this recipe. Sometimes I omit the olives and basil and use green peppers, carrots and hard boiled eggs.

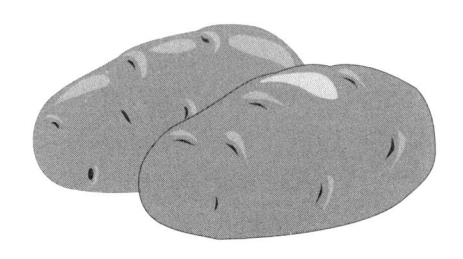

Mashed Potatoes and Spinach

4-5 lbs. mashed potatoes (cooked with skins or peeled)
1 bunch fresh spinach (washed and chopped) or 1 box of frozen spinach - drained
½ onion, grated fine (can substitute with onion powder)
sea salt and freshly ground pepper to taste
¼ cup grape seed oil (or more if mixture is too dry)

Mash potatoes with oil, sea salt and pepper. Add spinach and combine. Put into an oven pan and bake at 350° for about 20-30 minutes.

Try mashed potatoes and mashed turnips for another delicious combination.

Oven Roasted Home "Fried" Potatoes

I love home fries; in fact, my whole family does. Since I make them a lot, I have tried to find a way to make the potatoes quickly, tasty and with less butter/oil.
I hope you like this version.

4-5 lbs. potatoes
1 large red or white onion, chopped
2-3 leeks, chopped and washed
paprika
garlic powder
onion powder
parsley, fresh or dry

sea salt and freshly ground pepper to taste
1-2 tablespoons butter (optional)
¼ cup grape seed oil (start with less and add more if potatoes are too dry)

Preheat oven to 450°. Put butter into a large roasting pan, put the pan into the oven and melt the butter. Take the pan out, put the oil and seasonings into the pan and mix together. Use any type of potato you like, although the red skin and russet potatoes work very well. Leave the skins on or peel the potatoes. Cut the potatoes into chunks or slices. Place the potatoes, onions and leek into the pan and mix until they are well coated. I do not measure the seasonings except for the sea salt. I usually use 1-2 teaspoons of sea salt and a fair amount of paprika, garlic powder, ground pepper and parsley. Onion powder is optional. Adjust the seasonings to suit your taste. Place pan in oven and roast the potatoes until they are done. The cooking time varies depending upon the size of the potatoes. It takes about 45 minutes to cook the potatoes. Stir them every 15 minutes to allow for even cooking. We like our potatoes well done, so I cook them until they are very brown and crispy. You can cook these potatoes in a 350° oven and then broil them later in the cooking process, to make them crisp.

Potato Pancakes

- 1 tablespoon spelt or oat flour
- 1 tablespoon baking powder
- ¾ teaspoon sea salt
- ¼ teaspoon freshly ground pepper
- 2 eggs
- 1 medium/small onion, finely grated
- 6 potatoes, peeled and grated lengthwise by hand or electric grater. If using a hand held grater, use large holes and make long downward strokes. Squeeze potatoes to get water out.
- canola oil

Preheat oven to 550°. Grease a cookie pan with canola oil. Mix flour, baking powder, sea salt and freshly ground pepper. In a separate bowl, beat eggs and add to dry mixture. Add onion to mixture and stir. Add potatoes and mix. Depending upon the size of the pancake you want, drop a portion of the mixture onto the cookie pan and press it down a bit to form a pancake. Fill the pan, leaving space between each pancake. Put into oven for 8-10 minutes or until well browned and turn over. Reduce the oven temperature to 475° and bake another 10 minutes or until the second side is well browned. Serve immediately. Unsweetened applesauce is delicious with the pancakes.

Sweet Potatoes

There are so many ways to prepare sweet potatoes. Up until recently, I only ate them once a year on Thanksgiving Day. They were made with the usual brown sugar, maple syrup and the occasional marshmallow. The following recipes are much healthier and surprisingly delicious.

Sliced Sweet Potatoes

4-5 lbs. sweet potatoes
2 tablespoons sweet butter
2 tablespoons canola oil
3-4 tablespoons vanilla extract
1-2 tablespoons cinnamon
⅛ teaspoon sea salt

Preheat oven to 350°. Put butter in baking dish and put in oven until butter is just melted. Remove the pan from the oven, add oil, vanilla, and all seasonings and stir. Peel sweet potatoes and slice into ¼ inch pieces. Add potatoes to pan and mix to coat. Put into oven and bake about 20 minutes. Stir the potatoes every 10 minutes or so and continue to bake the potatoes for about 40 minutes or until they are tender. For a different taste, you can roast the potatoes with grape seed oil, sea salt and pepper. Try cutting the potatoes into different shapes and sizes. You can leave the skins on, it's your choice. You can use less oil and/or butter. The potatoes will be a bit dry, but just as good.

Sweet Potato Pudding

This recipe can be used with or without a pie crust. If you don't use a crust, grease a pie plate with a little butter or canola oil.

4 medium sweet potatoes (try different varieties of sweet potatoes)	⅛ teaspoon sea salt
	⅛ teaspoon nutmeg
	⅛ teaspoon allspice
	⅛ teaspoon ground cloves
1 egg (optional)	⅛ teaspoon ground ginger
2 tablespoons sweet butter, melted	¼-½ cup unsweetened coconut, lightly toasted (optional)
1 small container vanilla or plain soy or rice milk (8 oz)	2 teaspoons peach or apricot jam (sweetened with fruit juice) or
1 teaspoon cinnamon	¼ cup fresh orange juice
3 tablespoons vanilla extract	sweet butter

Preheat oven to 300°. Prick the potatoes and bake for about 1 ½-2 hours. Remove skin and mash potatoes. Put potatoes and all ingredients except the coconut into a food processor. Process until creamy. Lightly grease a pie plate with sweet butter. Pour mixture into the pie plate. Sprinkle coconut over top and lightly press it into the potato mixture. Bake pudding in a 350° oven for 35-40 minutes. This dish can be used as a main entree, side dish, dessert or snack. It also freezes well. Cut up the pudding into 6-8 servings, put each piece into a small self-sealing plastic bag and freeze. When you want to eat it, remove from the

Sweet Potato Pudding

freezer and reheat it in a 300-350° oven for about 20 minutes. This pudding may be used as a filling for a pie. Use the pie crust recipe on page 101. Bake the crust first, add the pudding and bake as indicated above.

For a vanilla flavored pudding, omit the allspice, ginger and cloves. Use ½ teaspoon of cinnamon and all the other ingredients.

If you can find organic white sweet potatoes, try them. I think they are delicious and they give this recipe a unique flavor. You will need to add more soy or rice milk because white sweet potatoes are fairly dry.

Roasted Root Vegetables

3	turnips	1	teaspoon garlic powder
4	carrots	1	bay leaf
1	rutabaga	1	teaspoon sea salt
3	parsnips	3	tablespoons grape seed oil
2	sweet potatoes	½	cup of water
2	white potatoes		freshly ground pepper
¼	teaspoon ground sage		to taste

Preheat oven to 350°. Cut up the root vegetables into chunks. Put them into a baking dish that has a lid. Sprinkle with seasonings, water and oil. Stir to coat the vegetables. Cover the mixture and put into the oven. Stir occasionally and adjust the seasonings if necessary. Cook for about one hour or until the vegetables are tender. All of these vegetables may not be available at any one time, so buy what you can and enjoy! This makes a delicious main entrée or side dish.

Summer Salad

- 1 medium green cabbage, washed and shredded
- 2-3 carrots, washed and thinly sliced
- 2-3 green peppers, washed and sliced
- 2-3 cucumbers, washed and sliced
- 2-3 medium Spanish onions, sliced
- 4 cloves of garlic, thinly sliced or finely chopped (or more to taste)
- ¼ cup canola oil
- ½ cup pineapple juice (sweetened with fruit juice)
- 2 teaspoons sea salt
- 1 lemon, juice only
- 1 lime, juice only
- 2 tablespoons water

Put all ingredients into a large bowl which has an air tight lid. Mix well, cover and refrigerate for 1-2 days. Stir occasionally. Adjust seasonings to your taste. Serve cold.

Butternut Squash Bake

- 1 large onion, peeled and cut into large pieces
- 1 butternut squash, peeled and cut into chunks
- ½ bag frozen cherries, thawed and drained (use fresh cherries when available, but be sure to remove the pits)
- 1 tablespoon grape seed oil
- ½ teaspoon sage
- ½ teaspoon sea salt
- freshly ground pepper to taste

Preheat oven to 425°. Toss onions with the oil and put into a medium sized oven proof dish. Cook the onions in the oven until browned. Add the rest of the ingredients to the onions and mix. Reduce the oven temperature to 350° and bake covered for about 30 minutes. The squash should be tender, but not soft. Adjust seasonings to your taste and serve. Delicious alone or with poultry.

Salad Dressings, Sauces and Marinades

For a quick salad dressing, use the following ingredients:

1-2 tablespoons olive oil
½ - 1 teaspoon sea salt
⅛ teaspoon oregano
½ teaspoon garlic powder
freshly ground pepper to taste
freshly squeezed lemon juice to taste
soy parmesan cheese to taste

Put all ingredients into your salad and mix to coat. Adjust seasonings to your taste.

Lemon Oil Salad Dressing

- 1 cup olive oil
- ¼ cup water
- ¼ cup fresh lemon juice
- 1 clove garlic, crushed (can use more if you like a strong garlic flavor)
- ¼ teaspoon oregano
- ½ tablespoon basil
- ¼ teaspoon thyme
- ¼ teaspoon sea salt
- freshly ground pepper to taste
- pinch of dry mustard
- pinch of ground celery seed

Blend all ingredients with a whisk or hand blender. Make a day or two ahead, the flavor will be more pronounced. Adjust the seasonings to your taste. This also makes a good marinade for fish and chicken.

Cathy's Marinara Sauce

My friend Cathy and I share recipes at times and this sauce is especially good and easy to make.

1	tablespoon grape seed oil	sea salt, freshly ground pepper, parsley (fresh or dried) and basil (fresh or dried) to taste
2	cloves garlic, chopped	
1	large can crushed tomatoes	

Using a toaster oven or regular oven, set at 300°, bake chopped garlic in 1 tablespoon oil until soft and remove from oven. Put all other ingredients into a large frying pan. Bring sauce to a boil, then lower heat, add the garlic and oil and simmer for about 40 minutes. This freezes well, so make a lot and store it in the freezer. Add a can of water packed tuna (drained) to this sauce and serve it over rice pasta for a quick and tasty meal.

Basic White Sauce

1	cup plain soy or rice milk	¼	cup sweet butter
1¼	cups water (for poultry or vegetable dishes you can use chicken stock instead of water)	¼	cup flour (use either spelt or oat flour)

Combine soy or rice milk and water or broth in a saucepan and slowly heat, but do not allow to boil. Melt butter in a medium saucepan, stir in flour and whisk over medium heat for 2-3 minutes. Then, slowly pour in heated soy milk/water into the butter and flour mixture, stirring constantly. Bring to a boil to thicken.

White Sauce (3 variations)

1, 2 or 3 tablespoons sweet butter

1, 2 or 3 tablespoons flour (use either spelt or oat flour)

1 cup plain soy or rice milk, heated

¼ teaspoon sea salt

pinch nutmeg (optional)

(If you use 1 tablespoon butter and 1 tablespoon flour, you will get a thin sauce. Using 2 tablespoons of each, you will get a medium thick sauce and if you use 3 tablespoons of each, you will get a thick sauce)

Melt butter in pan, stir in flour and cook 3 minutes over low to medium heat, stirring constantly. Add sea salt and nutmeg. Add soy or rice milk slowly, stirring constantly and bring to a boil to thicken. Set the pan over a very low heat or even in oven for a while - it will get richer and thicker. If the sauce lumps up, blend in a blender. Makes about 1 cup of sauce.

Sweet and Sour Sauce for Chicken or Tofu

Delicious and easy!

½ jar apricot jam (sweetened with fruit juice)

½ jar peach jam (sweetened with fruit juice)

1 tablespoon fresh lemon juice

1 teaspoon paprika

⅛ teaspoon sea salt

Mix all ingredients well. Brush on chicken or tofu, marinate for 1 hour and then bake, broil or grill.

Marinade for Chicken or Tofu

¼ cup peach jam (sweetened with fruit juice)
¼ cup apricot jam (sweetened with fruit juice)
2 teaspoons canola oil
½ - 1 teaspoon homemade mustard (page 12)
½ teaspoon sea salt
2 teaspoons fresh lemon juice

Mix all ingredients together in a small bowl. Spread the marinade on both sides of the tofu or chicken. Put in the refrigerator for a couple of hours. Grill or bake - it's your choice!

Marinade for Chicken, Fish or Tofu

2 tablespoons peach or apricot jam (sweetened with fruit juice)
1 teaspoon Bragg Liquid Aminos or 1 teaspoon fresh lemon juice
⅛ teaspoon mild curry
⅛ teaspoon paprika
pinch of cayenne
2-3 teaspoons of water

Mix all ingredients together except the water. Add the water a little at a time until you have the consistency of a sauce. You can make the sauce thinner by using more water or thicker by using less water. Spread on chicken, fish or tofu. Cook in the oven or on a grill.

Seafood Marinade

½ fresh squeezed lemon
1 tablespoon parsley, fresh or dried
1 tablespoon grape seed oil
½ teaspoon Bragg Liquid Aminos (optional)
⅛ teaspoon sea salt
freshly ground pepper to taste

Mix all ingredients and pour into a baking dish. Use scallops, halibut, flounder, shrimp, or any other type of fish you like. Cover and put into the refrigerator for about 1 hour. Broil in oven or grill.

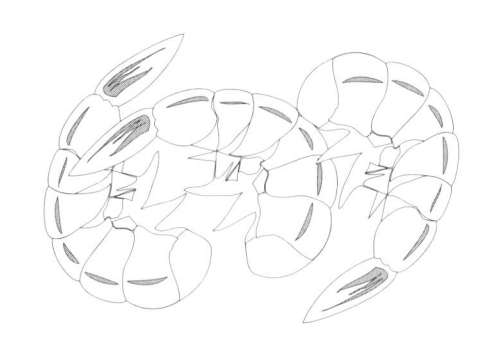

Poultry

Chicken Breasts

6 thinly sliced chicken breasts, bone and skin removed
2 eggs
water
homemade wheat-free bread crumbs, (page 88)
6 thin slices of onion
1 cup or more of chicken broth
2 teaspoons sweet butter
paprika, sea salt and freshly ground pepper to taste
1 jar of red raspberry jam (sweetened with fruit juice)

Preheat oven to 350°. Pat the breasts dry and pound flat. Mix the 2 eggs with 1 eggshell worth of water. Dip the breasts in egg mixture and then the bread crumbs, which have been mixed with the paprika, sea salt and pepper. Place a thin slice of onion on the breast and roll it up and secure with 2 toothpicks. Put in a baking dish, sprinkle with a little paprika and butter. Bake 15 minutes, until slightly browned and butter melted. Pour ½ cup of chicken broth into the pan. Bake 30-40 minutes more until chicken is done, occasionally basting with the broth. If dry, add more broth. The cooking time depends upon the thickness of the chicken breasts, so check them after 30 minutes.

Sauce

Use a jar of red raspberry jam, sweetened with fruit juice. Put the jam into a sauce pan and stir. Over low heat, warm the jam until it softens and reaches the consistency of a sauce. Use the sauce on top of the chicken when serving. Basmati rice and a salad go very well with this dish.

Chicken Fricassee

- 1   3 to 4 lb. chicken, cut up into (8) pieces
- 1   lb. ground chicken, shaped into small balls
- 2   teaspoons paprika
- 2   teaspoons sea salt
- ½   teaspoon pepper
- ⅛-¼ teaspoon sage
- 2-3 cloves of garlic, crushed
- 3   medium onions, chopped
- ½   cup boiling water or chicken stock

Mix the paprika, sea salt, pepper and crushed garlic into a paste and rub it onto the chicken parts. Brown the chicken parts in some chicken stock and remove. Then brown the chicken meatballs. Put all the chicken into the pot, add the onions, boiling water or chicken stock and sprinkle with sage. Simmer until tender.

Chicken Meatballs

1 lb. ground chicken
1½ cups chicken broth

garlic powder, onion powder, parsley, paprika, sea salt and freshly ground pepper to taste

Preheat oven to 350°. Mix all ingredients. Shape into balls. Place in a baking dish and bake for about 40 minutes or until browned. Serve the chicken meatballs with Italian tomato sauce or try this other variation. Slice onions and peppers, mix them with 1 tablespoon of grape seed oil, sea salt and pepper to taste and bake them in the oven until they are fairly soft. While the vegetables are cooking, prepare the chicken meatballs as indicated above. When the vegetables are soft, remove them from the oven and put the chicken meatballs into the oven to bake for about 20-30 minutes. Add the vegetables and 1½ cups of chicken broth to the chicken meatballs and bake for another 15-20 minutes. Serve with rice or pasta.

Chicken Pot Pie

3 to 4 lb. chicken, cut up
2 carrots, sliced
1 celery stalk, chopped
1 leek, sliced
1 cup of cauliflower, green beans or any other vegetable you like

garlic powder, onion powder, parsley, dill, thyme, sea salt and freshly ground pepper to taste
1 bay leaf

Use the oat biscuit recipe (page 85) or spelt muffin recipe (page 83) for the crust. Pour the batter into a fairly deep baking dish and bake at 425° for about 10 minutes until set and slightly brown. Take out of oven.

Make one recipe of the basic white sauce (page 47). Use the same flour for the white sauce that you use for the crust. Also, you can use chicken broth instead of water.

Put 3-4 lbs. of cut up chicken into a pot with water to cover. Add carrots, celery, leek, cauliflower and any other vegetable. Add garlic powder, onion powder, parsley, dill, thyme, bay leaf, sea salt and pepper to taste. Bring to a boil and then simmer until the chicken and carrots are tender. Remove chicken and vegetables from the water. Preheat oven to 350°. Remove the chicken from the bones and cut up. In a large bowl, mix the chicken, vegetables and white sauce and pour over biscuit mixture. Bake for about ½ hour. Save the chicken soup for another meal.

Madame A's Chicken in a Pan

- 4 boneless chicken cutlets, cut in strips and then in half
- 4 tablespoons apricot or peach jam (sweetened with fruit juice)
- 1 teaspoon mild curry
- ¼ teaspoon dry mustard
- ¼ teaspoon paprika
- ¼ teaspoon garlic powder
- sprinkle of cayenne powder (optional)
- sea salt and freshly ground pepper to taste
- 2 tablespoons arrowroot
- 1 ounce of cold water

Put a half inch of water into a large frying pan and bring it to a boil. Add chicken and boil until almost done, turning as needed. Combine the apricot jam, curry, dry mustard, paprika, garlic powder, cayenne powder, sea salt and freshly ground pepper into a paste. Mix the arrowroot with the water and add it to the paste and combine. Put the seasoning mixture into the pan with the chicken, mix and simmer for 30 minutes. Adjust the seasonings to your taste. You can add vegetables to this and make a chicken stew. Serve with basmati rice for a delicious meal.

Madame A's Lemon Garlic Chicken

- 4 chicken breasts with bone
- ½ cup of fresh lemon juice
- ½ cup chicken broth
- 1 small onion, finely chopped
- 2 cloves of garlic, finely chopped
- 1 tablespoon arrowroot mixed with 1 ounce of cold water
- sea salt and freshly ground pepper to taste

Turn broiler on. Put chicken breasts into a broiling pan and add water to cover two thirds of the chicken. Broil 15 minutes, turn and broil another 15 minutes. Turn oven down to 350°. Add all the other ingredients with enough liquid to completely cover the chicken. Bake for 1 hour .

Omelette in the Oven

1-2 eggs, beaten
½ teaspoon butter
pinch of salt
freshly ground pepper to taste

any other seasonings you like (try onion flakes, chives, garlic powder)
1 tablespoon shredded soy mozzarella or cheddar cheese (optional)

Preheat oven to 350°. Put the butter into a small baking dish. Place the dish in the oven until the butter melts. Remove the dish from the oven and tilt the dish to spread the butter along the sides and bottom. Add desired seasonings to the beaten egg(s) and mix. Pour the egg mixture into the dish and put it into the oven. Bake for about 10 minutes or until completely cooked. If you do not add any seasonings, try a little jam (sweetened with fruit juice) on top of the eggs.

Another variation: sprinkle ⅛ teaspoon cinnamon and a pinch of nutmeg into the beaten egg. Add ¼ teaspoon of your favorite extract (vanilla, orange, almond, etc.) and mix. Bake according to instructions.

Broccoli Quiche

- 1 bunch of fresh broccoli, steamed and finely chopped or 1 package of frozen chopped broccoli, defrosted and drained
- 8 ounces of plain soy or rice milk
- 1 egg
- ½ teaspoon sea salt
- freshly ground pepper to taste
- pinch of nutmeg or cinnamon (optional)
- 3 scallions, green part only, finely chopped
- 4 ounces Soya Kaas "Cheddar Cheese," shredded
- canola oil

Preheat oven to 350°. You can use a pie crust (page 101) or make this crustless. If you do not use a crust, lightly brush the pie plate with some canola oil. Clean and wash the broccoli. Cut it into small pieces, put it into a pot of boiling water and steam for two minutes. Drain the broccoli and chop it into fairly small pieces. Put the soy or rice milk, egg, sea salt, pepper and nutmeg or cinnamon into a food processor and blend for about 30 seconds. Pour milk mixture into a large bowl. Add the broccoli, scallions, and "Cheddar Cheese" and mix with a large spoon. Pour mixture into a lightly greased pie plate and bake for about 30-40 minutes.

Spinach Quiche

- 2 eggs
- 8 ounces plain soy or rice milk
- 1 tablespoon arrowroot
- 1 package frozen chopped spinach, thawed and well drained (or 1 lb. fresh spinach, cleaned and chopped)
- 1 package of fresh mushrooms, cleaned and chopped or sliced
- 3 scallions, green part only, chopped
- 4 ounces soy "mozzarella cheese," shredded
- ½ - ¾ teaspoon sea salt to taste
- ⅛ teaspoon cinnamon
- pinch of nutmeg (optional)
- freshly ground pepper to taste
- canola oil

Preheat oven to 350°. You can use a pie crust (page 101) or make it crustless. If you do not use a crust, lightly brush the pie plate with canola oil. Put eggs, soy or rice milk and arrowroot into a large mixing bowl and blend with a whisk or electric beater. Add spinach, mushrooms, scallions, cheese and seasonings and mix with a spoon. Pour mixture into a pre-baked pie crust or into a lightly greased pie plate and bake for 45 minutes to 1 hour.

Ground Turkey

Use ground turkey as a substitute for ground beef. It is delicious and lower in fat. You can get ground dark meat or white meat turkey.

Turkey Chili

- 3 lbs. ground turkey
- 2 cups kidney beans, cooked **(see page 72)** or 1 can, rinsed and drained
- 2 cups pinto beans, cooked **(see page 72)** or 1 can, rinsed and drained
- 1 can refried beans (optional, but I like it because it makes the sauce thicker)
- 2 large cans of crushed tomatoes or chunky tomato sauce
- 1 onion, chopped
- 2-3 leeks, washed, drained and chopped (use the whole leek)
- 1 green pepper, chopped (optional)
- 2 cloves of garlic, chopped
- chili powder or a sprinkle of dried chili pepper flakes, cumin, garlic powder, oregano, coriander, allspice, cloves, paprika, sea salt,
- fresh lemon juice and freshly ground pepper to taste

Brown turkey meat, breaking into small pieces. Drain any fat. Add all other ingredients and simmer for about 1 hour. If you are not able to eat tomatoes, use chicken broth.

Turkey Meat Loaf

- 1 medium onion, finely chopped
- 1 celery stalk, finely chopped
- 1 green or red pepper, finely chopped
- 1 carrot, finely chopped
- 1 zucchini, finely chopped
- 4 lbs. ground turkey
- 1 teaspoon sea salt
- freshly ground pepper to taste
- garlic powder to taste
- 1-2 eggs (optional)
- 1 tablespoon parsley
- 1 can tomato paste (optional)
- a little water

Preheat oven to 350°. Sauté the vegetables in a little water (about ¼ cup). Use any or all of the vegetables I have suggested or get creative and use whatever else you think would be good in the loaf. Mix the turkey, vegetables and all other ingredients except the tomato paste. Form the meat mixture into one or two loaves and put into a baking dish. Mix tomato paste with some water to achieve the consistency of tomato soup. Spread the tomato paste onto the top and sides of the loaf. Bake for 1-1½ hours or until done.

Turkey Meatballs and Italian Gravy

Turkey Meatballs

- 3 lbs. ground turkey
- 1 egg (optional)
- sea salt and freshly ground pepper to taste
- 2-3 cloves garlic, sliced
- ½ cup homemade wheat-free bread crumbs (page 88)
- 1 teaspoon garlic powder
- 1 teaspoon onion powder
- ½ teaspoon oregano
- ½ teaspoon basil
- ¼ cup fresh parsley, chopped
- ¼-½ cup water

Preheat oven to 350°. Mix all ingredients together. Shape into balls and put into a baking dish. Put the slices of garlic into the pan. Bake until browned. Put the turkey meatballs into the Italian gravy.

Gravy

- 2 large cans of tomato purée
- 2 large cans of crushed tomatoes
- 2 small cans tomato paste
- basil, oregano, parsley, sea salt and freshly ground pepper to taste
- 12 oz. of water

Put all ingredients into a large pot and mix. Add turkey meatballs and simmer for at least 1 hour. You can also add turkey sausage, which has been browned first.

Italian Meat Sauce

- 3 lbs. ground turkey
- 1-2 turkey sausage links- Cut up into pieces or remove from casing and break up into little pieces
- 3 large cans tomatoes - use a variety of purée, crushed, whole, etc.
- 2 6 oz. cans tomato paste
- 12 oz. of water
- 1 whole onion- peel, throw in whole and remove after cooking or coarsely chop
- parsley, basil, oregano, sea salt and freshly ground pepper to taste (use fresh herbs if possible)
- 2 cloves garlic, crushed

Brown ground turkey and sausage. Drain fat. Add all ingredients and stir. Simmer for about 1½ hours.

Lasagne

This recipe works so well, that people do not realize it is not "regular" lasagne. Try it, I know you will like it!

- 1 box rice lasagne noodles Italian meat sauce (page 63) or marinara sauce (page 47)
- 1 8 ounce package of Soya Kaas "Mozzarella Cheese," shredded
- 1 package of firm tofu, drained
- 2 tablespoons of Soya Kaas "Parmesan Cheese" plus some extra for sprinkling between layers
- 1 egg
- ¼ - ½ cup plain soy or rice milk
- 1 tablespoon of fresh chopped parsley or dried parsley
- ½ teaspoon sea salt
- freshly ground pepper to taste

Make turkey meat sauce or marinara sauce and set aside. Cook rice noodles according to the directions on the box. Rice pasta is a bit difficult to work with, so be patient. Sometimes the noodles break apart, but the broken pieces work just as well as the whole pieces. Drain and lay out on wax paper. Drain the tofu and cut it into chunks. Put the tofu, 2 tablespoons soy " Parmesan cheese," egg, milk, parsley, sea salt and pepper into a food processor. Cream the ingredients until they are the consistency of ricotta cheese. Set aside about ½ cup of "mozzarella cheese" for the top of the lasagne and then add the remaining "mozzarella cheese" to the tofu mixture and combine. Preheat oven to 350°. Put sauce in the bottom of a 9x13 baking dish and spread it around. Add a layer of noodles, then tofu mixture, then a layer of sauce and sprinkle a little bit of "Parmesan cheese" on top. Repeat until you use up all the lasagne noodles. Put remaining soy "mozzarella cheese" on the top layer and sprinkle with some soy "Parmesan cheese." Bake about 1 hour.

Seafood

I love fish and eat it fairly often. Experiment with different fresh or dried herbs. Broil, grill, bake, poach, or steam the fish.

Baked Fish Fillets

4 fish fillets (I have used halibut, but scrod, flounder, cod and other meaty white fish would work well with this recipe)	½ cup soy or rice milk, warm, but not boiling ½ teaspoon sea salt homemade wheat-free bread crumbs (page 88) 2 tablespoons sweet butter

Preheat oven to 550°. Melt 1 tablespoon of butter in baking pan and brush it to coat the entire bottom of the pan. Melt another 1-2 tablespoons of butter in a separate pan and set aside. Wash and dry fillets. Heat the milk until it is warm, but not boiling. Put some bread crumbs onto a plate or piece of wax paper. Put the warm milk and sea salt into a pie plate and stir to mix. Dip the fish into the milk mixture and then into the bread crumbs. Put the fish into the baking dish and pour melted butter over the fillets. Place on top shelf of oven and bake 10 minutes or until done. Be careful not to overcook the fish. The high temperature cooks the fish quickly and yet the fillets remain moist.

Baked Salmon

2 salmon fillets (about 6 ounces each), rinsed and dried with paper toweling
1½ tablespoons lime juice
1½ tablespoons apricot or peach jam (sweetened with fruit juice)
1 tablespoon grape seed oil
sea salt and freshly ground pepper to taste

Put salmon in an oven proof dish, skin side down. Combine all other ingredients and brush onto salmon. Cover and refrigerate for 30 minutes. Preheat oven to 450°. Bake salmon for 15 minutes or until cooked through. The fish should flake easily when tested with a fork. Try other seasonings such as curry, cayenne powder, garlic powder, etc. to spice it up!

Broiled, Baked or Grilled Salmon

Season the salmon with some melted butter, and a little bit of sea salt, pepper, paprika, parsley, garlic powder, onion powder, ground celery seed. Cook the fish any way you like.

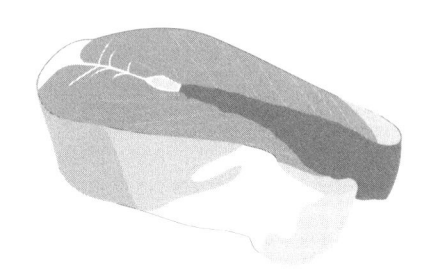

Scallops, Spinach, Mushrooms and Garlic

- 2 lbs. of fresh spinach, washed and drained, leave whole
- 4 cloves garlic, peeled and sliced
- 1 lb. fresh mushrooms, cleaned and sliced
- ¼ cup of water
- 2 tablespoons grape seed oil
- 1½ teaspoons Bragg Liquid Aminos
- 2 teaspoons fresh lemon juice
- ½ teaspoon sea salt
- freshly ground pepper to taste
- 1 lb. sea scallops, sliced into thin rounds

Preheat oven to 350°. Steam spinach, keep it covered and set aside. Put the sliced garlic and mushrooms into an oven proof dish. Add the water and oil and stir. Put vegetables into the oven and cook for about 5-10 minutes, stirring once. Turn the oven up to 500°. Add the Bragg Liquid Aminos, lemon juice, sea salt, freshly ground pepper and scallops to the mushroom and garlic mixture. Put the dish back into the oven and cook for 3-5 minutes or until scallops are done. Be careful not to overcook the fish. Put spinach on a plate and fish mixture on top of the spinach. Serve immediately.

Tofu

I remember buying my first package of tofu and putting it in the back of my dairy draw in the refrigerator. It stayed there until it expired. I was scared to try it. What if I spent two hours preparing a meal with it and no one in my family liked it? I didn't want to have to throw away the meal and make something else. I was also resistant to trying something new. A few weeks later, I bought another package and this time I gathered the courage to cook it. I'm glad I took the plunge. Tofu is a wonderfully versatile food. It is a source of protein, so begin to use it as a substitute for chicken, poultry and cheese. Be aware that tofu has a texture unlike other proteins. It is soft and moist. Virtually tasteless, tofu absorbs the flavor of the other ingredients in the dish. You can bake, broil, grill, roast and sauté it. You can cream, crumble, dice, slice and mash it. Today I eat it for breakfast, as a snack and in main entrées.

Breakfast Tofu

- 1 package firm tofu, drained and sliced into 4 pieces
- ¼ cup peach jam (sweetened with fruit juice)
- ¼ cup apricot jam (sweetened with fruit juice)
- ¼ cup pineapple juice (sweetened with fruit juice)
- ¼ teaspoon orange flavor, alcohol free
- ⅛ teaspoon cinnamon
- pinch of salt
- unsweetened, shredded coconut (optional)

Preheat oven to 350°. Lay the tofu slices in a baking dish. In a small bowl, mix peach jam, apricot jam, pineapple juice, orange flavor, cinnamon and sea salt together until smooth.

Cont'd

Breakfast Tofu

Brush sauce over tofu. Turn the slices over and brush sauce on the other side. Sprinkle a little coconut over the slices. Place the baking dish in oven and bake for 30 minutes. Turn the slices over and bake another 20-30 minutes. To achieve a crispy texture after baking, put the slices under the broiler for a few minutes.

Experiment with other flavors such as maple, almond and butterscotch. You can put a little bit of sweet butter on top of each slice. This recipe is a great substitute for French toast.

Italian Tofu Stew

- 2 packages of firm tofu, drained and cut into large chunks
- 1 green or red pepper, chopped
- 1 medium onion, chopped
- 2 small zucchini, chopped
- 2 small yellow squash, chopped
- 1 package mushrooms, chopped
- 1-2 cloves garlic, crushed
- 1 teaspoon sea salt
- 1 large can crushed tomatoes or purée tomatoes
- chicken or vegetable broth

Heat a large saucepan, add about ½ cup of broth and heat. Add the tofu and sauté it until lightly browned. It may stick, but don't worry, just turn the heat down a little or add more liquid. Remove the tofu from the pan. Put other ingredients into the pan and simmer until vegetables are soft. Add tofu to the vegetables, warm for a few minutes and serve.

Tofu Chili

- 1 package of firm tofu, drained and crumbled
- 2 medium onions, chopped
- 2-3 cloves of garlic, crushed
- 2 cups kidney beans, cooked **(see page 72)** or 1 can, rinsed and drained
- 2 cups pinto beans, cooked **(see page 72)** or 1 can, rinsed and drained
- 2 large cans of either crushed tomatoes or purée tomatoes (use chicken or vegetable broth to replace tomatoes)
- sea salt, paprika, cayenne, oregano, coriander, chili pepper flakes, cumin and tumeric to taste (be careful with the cayenne, it's very hot)
- ¼ cup unsweetened pineapple juice (optional)

Put all ingredients together in a large saucepan and simmer for about 1 hour.

Tofu Spinach Pie

This recipe can be made with or without a pie crust. Use the pie crust recipe on page 101, using whichever flour you prefer. Bake the pie shell for 15-20 minutes and remove from the oven.

1	lb. fresh spinach, cleaned, washed and chopped or 1 package frozen spinach, thawed and drained	4-5	mushrooms, finely chopped
2-3	tablespoons chicken or vegetable stock	1	lb. soft tofu, (creamed in food processor)
1	small onion, finely chopped	½	teaspoon sea salt
		½	teaspoon cinnamon
		¼	cup plain soy or rice milk
		1	egg, beaten (optional)
			canola oil

Preheat oven to 400°. Over low heat, sauté onion in stock until soft. Add spinach and mushrooms and sauté for 2 minutes. Mix onion, spinach, mushrooms, tofu, milk, egg and seasonings. Spoon mixture into the pre-baked pie shell and bake for about 30 minutes or until crust is golden. If you do not use a pie crust, lightly grease the pie plate with canola oil.

Dried Beans & Lentils

I never imagined that I would be eating all types of beans, but I do and I ENJOY them! Beans are easy to prepare, so use fresh beans as much as possible. My favorite way to eat beans is to cook some garlic, onion and peppers and then add the beans and eat. They make a delicious meal or side dish. Try them all to see which are your favorites. Don't forget to use them in soups, chili and salads. Beans also freeze well, so cook some up, and freeze them until you need them for soup or chili, etc.

If I need 2 cups of cooked beans, I start with ¾ cups raw beans. Rinse the beans. Put them in a large pot with 3 to 4 times their volume of water. Cover and soak overnight. For a quicker soaking method, bring them to a boil and let stand off the heat, covered for an hour or two. After soaking the beans, drain the water and fill the pot with new water about double the volume of beans. Bring water to a boil, then lower heat to a gentle simmer. Cover and leave lid slightly ajar to prevent foaming. Cook slowly and thoroughly. Bite into a bean to decide when it is thoroughly cooked. This is a personal choice. If you want to add sea salt, do so only after cooking the beans. Using a pressure cooker will decrease the amount of cooking time.

Cooking Times

Black Beans . . . . 1½ hours
Black Eyed Peas . . . . 1-1¼ hours
Chickpeas (Garbanzo Beans) . . . . 2½-3 hours
Cannelloni Beans . . . . 1½-2 hours
Kidney or Red Beans . . . . 1½-2 hours
Navy Beans . . . . 1-1½ hours
Pinto Beans . . . . 1½-2 hours
Brown Lentils . . . . 45 minutes
Red Lentils . . . . 30 minutes

"Baked Beans"

I call these baked beans because they taste very similar to the baked beans I used to eat. This recipe is quick and easy to make.

- 2 cups navy, great northern, pinto or whatever beans you like - cooked, **(see page 72)** or 1 can, rinsed and drained
- 2 tablespoons peach or apricot jam (sweetened with fruit juice)
- ¼ cup pineapple juice (sweetened with fruit juice)
- ⅛ teaspoon fresh lemon juice
- 1-2 tablespoons tomato paste
- ½ teaspoon dry mustard
- ½ teaspoon onion flakes
- ½ teaspoon sea salt
- ⅛ teaspoon ground celery root or seed
- ⅛ teaspoon onion powder
- ¼-½ teaspoon maple extract
- pinch of cayenne powder (optional)

Combine all ingredients in a saucepan and bring to a boil. Lower the temperature and simmer for about 10 minutes. Adjust seasonings to your taste.

Black Beans

2-4 tablespoons soup stock
1 cup onion, chopped
1 green or red pepper, chopped
3 cloves garlic, minced
4 cups cooked or canned black beans (about 1½ to 1⅔ cups raw, cooked) **(see page 72)**
juice of ½ lemon or more to taste
1 teaspoon ground cumin
¼ cup fresh parsley, chopped
sea salt and freshly ground pepper to taste

Heat stock in a large saucepan. Add the onion and pepper and sauté over moderate heat until soft. Add the garlic and cumin and sauté until the onion is golden. Add the beans along with about ½ cup of liquid from the can or from cooking. Bring to a simmer. Mash some of the beans with the back of a wooden spoon, enough to thicken the liquid. Add the remaining ingredients and simmer on very low heat for 10-15 minutes, then serve. You can use any kind of bean or try with brown lentils. Try Italian herbs for a change of flavor.

Chickpea Pancakes

- 3 cups garbanzo beans (chickpeas), cooked **(see page 72)** or 2 cans, rinsed and drained
- 1 egg
- ⅓ cup green pepper, finely chopped
- ⅓ cup onion, finely chopped
- 2-3 teaspoons minced garlic
- ½ cup chickpea flour
- 1¼ teaspoons sea salt
- 1¼ teaspoons cumin
- grape seed oil

Turn broiler on high. Place oven rack on middle shelf. Generously grease a broiler pan with oil. Put the chickpeas into a food processor and blend until they are crumbly. Put the chickpeas into a large mixing bowl. Add all the other ingredients and combine. Spoon the mixture into a ½ cup container, then gently drop the batter onto the broiler pan and shape into a pancake. Repeat until you use up the mixture. Put broiler pan into the oven. Broil for about 15-20 minutes until brown. Turn and cook another 5-10 minutes. The pancakes should be brown on both sides and not too dry inside. Try using other seasonings such as curry to vary the flavor. Another good combination is carrots, onions, garlic and fresh parsley. Try this or make up your own creation. These pancakes freeze well.

Gertie's Chili

My Dutch friend made this dish for me and I loved it.
I hope you do too!

- ¼ cup water or soup stock, or more as needed
- 1 onion, chopped
- 1 green pepper, chopped
- 2 cloves of garlic, chopped
- 3 leeks, chopped and rinsed (use the whole leek)
- 1 large can of chopped tomatoes
- 2 cups pinto beans, cooked **(see page 72)** or 1 can, rinsed and drained
- 2 cups kidney beans, cooked **(see page 72)** or 1 can, rinsed and drained
- 1 package mushrooms, cleaned and chopped
- 2-3 oz. pineapple juice (sweetened with fruit juice)
- chili powder, paprika, thyme and sea salt to taste

In a large pot, sauté the onion, green pepper, garlic and leek in the water or stock. Add the tomatoes and simmer. Then add the beans, mushrooms, pineapple juice and seasonings and simmer until well heated (about 20 minutes).

Lentil Loaf

- 5 cups lentils, cooked **(see page 72)** or 3 cans, rinsed and drained
- 1 small onion, finely chopped
- 1 green pepper, finely chopped
- 1 clove of garlic, finely chopped
- ½ cup homemade wheat-free bread crumbs (page 88)
- 1 8 ounce can tomato sauce or 1 small can of tomato paste mixed with water to achieve the consistency of tomato sauce (optional)
- 1 egg (optional)
- 1 teaspoon sea salt
- freshly ground pepper to taste
- grape seed oil

Preheat oven to 350°. Lightly grease a loaf pan with oil. Put lentils into a food processor and cream. Add all other ingredients and mix well. Treat this mixture like ground beef. Put lentil mixture into the loaf pan and shape the mixture to fit the pan. Spread tomato sauce over the top of the lentil loaf. Bake for about 1 hour.

Refried Beans

1	lb. pinto beans, raw	4	cloves garlic, sliced
1	large onion	1	tablespoon canola oil

Put beans in pot with twice as much water. Bring to a boil. Turn heat off, cover and let sit overnight. Next day, drain water and add new water (twice as much as beans). Bring to a boil, simmer until very soft (about 1½-2 hours). While beans are cooking, sauté the onion, and a little cumin in some water or chicken broth. Sauté until soft and remove from pan. Put sliced garlic into a small oven dish with 1 tablespoon of canola oil. Put it into a toaster oven and cook it at 300° until it is soft. Add garlic to onions. Take beans out and save the water. Leaving some beans whole put the rest of the beans, onions and garlic together and mash or use a food processor. Add sea salt, pepper, paprika, oregano or any other herb. Add water from beans to thin mixture. This freezes well, so make a large portion.

Aurora's Spanish Black Beans

- 1 lb. black beans, raw or canned **(see page 72)**
- ½ green pepper, diced
- ½ onion, diced
- 1-2 teaspoons oregano, crushed
- 2 bay leaves
- sea salt and freshly ground pepper to taste
- water

If using raw beans, rinse the beans and put them into a pot. Add water to the pot so that it is 2 inches above the beans. Put the lid on the pot and let beans soak overnight. Next day, drain the beans and put them back in the pot with fresh water. Bring water to a boil and then simmer for about 1½ hours. When beans start to get soft, add green pepper, onion, oregano, bay leaves, sea salt and pepper. Add water as needed. Cook until beans are soft, about 1 hour more.

Aurora's Spanish Kidney Beans

- 1 lb. kidney beans, raw
- ½ can tomato sauce
- ½ green pepper, chopped
- ½ onion, chopped
- 2 cloves garlic, minced or crushed
- sea salt and freshly ground pepper to taste

Put beans into a pot with water 2 inches over the beans and cover. Leave overnight. Next day, drain the beans and put them back in the pot with fresh water. Bring to a boil and then simmer for a couple of hours. When beans start to get soft, add tomato sauce, green pepper, onion, garlic, sea salt and pepper. Cook until beans are soft, about 1 hour more. Add water as needed.

Grains

1 Cup Grain	Liquid	Amount of time
Barley	3 cups	45 min-1 hour
Basmati Rice (brown)	2¼ cups	40-45 min
Basmati Rice (white)	1¾ cups	15-20 min
Long Grain Rice	2 cups	25-30 min
Millet	1½ cups	20 min
Pearl Barley	2½ cups	40 min

If still crunchy, add ¼ cup more water and simmer 10 minutes more. Fluff with a fork and let the grain sit, uncovered for 5-10 minutes before serving. A cup of raw grain yields 3 cups cooked grain and serves 4 people. There are other grains such as spelt berries, buckwheat, etc. Ask about them in your health food store.

White Basmati Rice

1 cup rice
1¾ cups water

1 tablespoon butter (optional)
½ teaspoon sea salt (optional)

Rinse and drain rice. Bring water to a boil. Stir in rice, butter and sea salt. Return to a boil, cover and simmer on low heat for 15-20 minutes until water is absorbed. Fluff with a fork. Let rice sit uncovered for 5-10 minutes. You can add herbs such as tumeric, chives, garlic powder, thyme to the rice. Also add vegetables such as cooked mushrooms or peas. Be creative!

Breads & Pancakes

Read the information on page 7 describing the different types of flour that I use.

Oat Flour Bread

- 2 cups oat flour
- 1 tablespoon baking powder
- ½ teaspoon sea salt
- 2 eggs, beaten
- 2 tablespoons unsweetened applesauce
- ¾ cup plain soy or rice milk

Preheat oven to 425°. Stir dry ingredients together, pressing out lumps. Mix liquids together and then add to dry mixture. Stir lightly. Pour into greased loaf pan. Bake for 20 minutes.

Rice Baking Mix Bread

- 2½ cups Fearn Rice Baking Mix
- 1¾ cups plain soy or rice milk
- 2 eggs, slightly beaten
- 2 tablespoons canola oil

Preheat oven to 400°. Combine soy or rice milk, eggs and oil. Add baking mix and stir until fairly smooth. Pour into a lightly oiled one pound loaf pan and bake for 1 hour. For variety, add blueberries, other fruit, sunflower seeds, etc.

Spelt Muffins

3 cups spelt flour
1 teaspoon baking powder
1 teaspoon sea salt

2 tablespoons sweet butter, melted
1⅓ cups plain soy or rice milk

Preheat oven to 350°. Grease one or two cookie pans with sweet butter. Mix dry ingredients. Blend liquids in a separate bowl. Combine mixtures. Batter should be like thick oatmeal. This dough is sticky and a little difficult to work with, so be patient. Drop ¼ cup of dough at a time onto the cookie pan. Continue until you use up all the dough. Bake for 35 minutes or until browned. This recipe makes about 10 biscuits.

Instead of making muffins, you can spread the entire batter evenly in the pan. Then when it is done baking, you can cut the bread into squares. Be sure to grease the pan well to make it easier to get the bread out.

Rice Baking Mix Muffins

2 cups Fearn Rice Baking Mix
2 eggs
4 tablespoons unsweetened applesauce

1½ cups plain soy or rice milk
vanilla, cinnamon, (optional)

Preheat oven to 400°. Put rice mix into a large mixing bowl. In a small bowl, beat eggs, add applesauce, milk and seasonings and mix. Add to rice mixture and stir until fairly smooth. Pour into muffin tin and bake for 20 minutes. Makes 12 muffins.

Barley Biscuits

- 1 cup brown rice flour
- 1 cup barley flour
- ½ teaspoon sea salt
- 4 teaspoons baking powder
- 4 tablespoons unsweetened applesauce
- 2 eggs
- 1 cup plain soy or rice milk

Preheat oven to 425°. Mix dry ingredients in a large bowl. Mix wet ingredients in a smaller, separate bowl and then pour into dry ingredients and mix. Spoon onto greased cookie sheets, forming a biscuit shape. Bake about 12 minutes or until lightly browned. Makes about 12 biscuits.

Oat Biscuits

- 2 cups oat flour or 1½ cups oat flour and ½ cup oat bran
- ½ teaspoon sea salt
- 4 teaspoons baking powder
- 4 tablespoons unsweetened applesauce
- 2 eggs
- 1 cup plain soy or rice milk

Preheat oven to 425°. Mix dry ingredients. Mix wet ingredients and stir into dry mixture. Spoon batter onto a lightly greased pan. (You can also pour the entire batter onto a lightly greased pan and bake as one whole piece and then cut it up after baking.) The recipe makes about 12 biscuits. Bake 12 minutes or until the biscuits are lightly browned. Place biscuits on a plate and let them cool.

Rice Baking Mix Pancakes

1 cup Fearn Rice Baking Mix
1 egg
1 tablespoon unsweetened applesauce
1 cup plain soy or rice milk

In a large bowl, combine egg, applesauce and soy or rice milk. Slowly add rice mix. Mix until fairly smooth. Do not over mix. Let batter stand for a few minutes. Then spoon onto a very lightly oiled hot pan. Turn once. When I make these, I make a lot and freeze them. A triple recipe fills a large self-sealing plastic bag. Take 3-4 pancakes and wrap them in wax paper to make it easier to remove them. Put them in the toaster oven to defrost and heat. They are delicious with fruit spread or fresh fruit.

Oat Flour Pancakes

1 cup oat flour
2½ teaspoons baking powder
½ teaspoon sea salt
1 egg
½ cup plain soy or rice milk
½ cup water
1 tablespoon unsweetened applesauce
¼ bag frozen blueberries, etc. (optional)

Stir dry ingredients in a large bowl, pressing out lumps. Blend egg, water, soy or rice milk and applesauce and beat well. Add wet ingredients to the dry ingredients and mix well. Drop by tablespoons onto hot, lightly greased pan. A triple recipe fills a large self-sealing plastic bag. Use wax paper because these pancakes are thin and difficult to get apart when frozen.

Barley Pancakes

¼ cup brown rice flour
¾ cup barley flour
1½ teaspoons baking powder
½ teaspoon sea salt
1 tablespoon canola oil
1 egg, beaten
1¾ cups plain soy or rice milk

Put ingredients into mixing bowl in listed order. Quickly whip or stir to a smooth consistency. Spoon onto a lightly greased, hot pan and cook until light brown and puffy.

Rice Baking Mix Waffles

1 cup Fearn Rice Baking Mix
1 egg, separated
2 tablespoons canola oil
1 scant cup plain soy or rice milk

Preheat waffle iron. Separate egg whites and beat until soft peaks form, not dry. Combine yolks, milk and oil in a large bowl. Add rice mix gradually and stir until fairly smooth. Fold in egg whites. Bake in hot waffle iron

Rice Waffles

1 cup brown rice flour
1 teaspoon baking powder
½ teaspoon sea salt
1 cup plain soy or rice milk
1 egg, separated
½ tablespoon sweet butter, melted

Sift dry ingredients in a bowl. Add egg yolk and soy or rice milk to the dry ingredients and beat together thoroughly. Beat egg whites until stiff, stir ¼ of whites into batter to lighten it and then gently fold in the rest of the egg whites. Put into waffle iron and bake.

Homemade Chips

Use spelt bread, rye bread or any other bread that you are allowed to eat. Spread a little butter or grape seed oil on bread and sprinkle on garlic powder, onion powder, oregano, sea salt, pepper and soy Parmesan cheese. Cut up into bite size pieces and toast until brown. Put into an airtight container to store. Delicious alone or with dips. Break up the crackers and use a croutons in soup or salads.

Homemade Wheat-Free Bread Crumbs

You can use any type of wheat and yeast-free bread you like. Choose from French Meadow's yeast-free spelt and rye bread or Ener G's white rice yeast-free loaf. Use one type of bread or mix one or two kinds together. If you use a Vita Mixer, just put chunks of fresh or frozen bread into the dry container and blend on high until you get the consistency you want. A food processor or mini food chopper can make bread crumbs as well. Put the bread crumbs onto a cookie pan and bake them in a 350° oven. Stir the bread crumbs occasionally until they are light brown and crispy. Use on chicken, fish or in any recipe that calls for bread crumbs. Store in an air tight container or freeze them.

Perfect Snack

Use raw hulled sunflower seeds or pumpkin seeds. Preheat oven to 320°. Put seeds into a shallow baking pan and roast for 10 minutes. Check and stir the seeds. Roast another 5 minutes, stir and roast 3-5 minutes more or until lightly browned. After roasting the seeds, put them into an airtight container. Add a small amount of sea salt and shake. For a different taste, sprinkle the seeds with garlic powder. They are delicious. You can buy these seeds in bulk or in individual packages.

Desserts

There <u>is</u> life after choosing not to use sugar. These recipes are wonderful substitutes for the desserts you are used to eating. They are not sugary sweet, but they are very satisfying. Use organic jams, which have been sweetened with fruit juice, unsweetened applesauce, unsweetened apple butter and flavoring extracts to create delicious and healthy desserts.

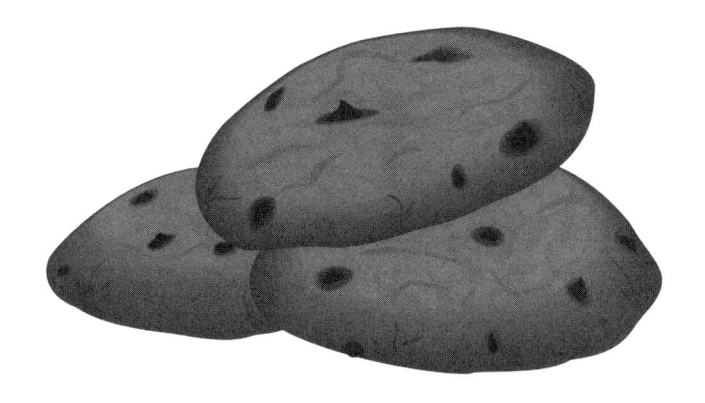

Banana Cake or Apple Cake

- 1 cup barley flour
- 1 cup brown rice flour
- 2 teaspoons baking powder
- 2 teaspoons baking soda
- ¾ teaspoon cinnamon
- ¼ teaspoon nutmeg
- 1 egg
- 1 stick sweet butter, softened
- 1 teaspoon vanilla extract
- 3 tablespoons unsweetened applesauce
- 3-4 ripe bananas, mashed
- canola oil

Preheat oven to 350°. Lightly grease baking dish with canola oil. You can use a square, loaf, or regular cake pan. In a small bowl, sift the barley and brown rice flour, baking powder, baking soda, cinnamon, and nutmeg. In a large bowl, on medium speed, cream butter, add banana and mix. Then add egg, vanilla and applesauce. Add flour mixture and mix at low speed until combined. Put in pan and bake for 25-30 minutes.
* Peel ripe bananas and freeze them in self-sealing plastic bags. They will get brown, but they become very sweet and are perfect for baking.

For Apple Cake

Omit the bananas and include the following:

- 2 apples peeled and chopped
- 1½ cups unsweetened applesauce
- ½ cup unsweetened apple butter
- 2 tablespoons peach or apricot jam (sweetened with fruit juice)
- ½ bag frozen blueberries, defrosted (optional)

One reader suggested warming up some soy or rice milk and pouring it over this cake to moisten it and make it more like bread pudding.

Carrot Cake

The original recipe called for two cups of sugar in the cake and ⅓ - ½ box of confectioners' sugar in the icing. Here is a healthier version of this cake.

- 1¼ cups oat flour
- ¾ cup barley flour
- 2 teaspoons baking powder
- 1 teaspoon sea salt
- 2 teaspoons cinnamon
- ¾ cup unsweetened apple butter
- ½ cup apricot or peach jam (sweetened with fruit juice)
- 4 eggs
- 1 pound of raw carrots, peeled and finely shredded
- canola oil

Preheat oven to 300°. Use canola oil to grease a 9 X 13 pan. Put the oat flour and barley flour into a sifter. Sift once and then put the flour back into the sifter and add the baking powder, sea salt and cinnamon and sift. Set aside. Using an electric beater on low speed, blend the apple butter, jam and eggs. Add the dry ingredients to the wet mixture and combine. Add the shredded carrots and mix. Pour into the baking pan and bake 1 hour or until a cake tester comes out clean. Let the cake cool before icing.

If you want to make a two layer cake double this recipe. Generously grease the bottom and sides of two cake pans with canola oil. Divide the batter between the two pans. Bake 50-60 minutes or until a cake tester comes out clean. Let the cake cool before icing. To remove the cake from the layer cake pan, slide a knife between the cake and the pan to carefully loosen the edges. Then gently slide the

Cont'd

Carrot Cake

knife under the cake to loosen it from the bottom of the pan. Put a dinner plate over the cake pan and gently shake the pan until the cake falls out of the pan and onto the plate.

Soy "Cream Cheese" Icing

The following soy "cream cheese" icing recipe covers a one layer cake. Double the recipe when making a two layer cake.

- 1 container of Soya Kaas plain cream cheese
- 1 ounce vanilla soy or rice milk
- ½ stick sweet butter, softened
- 2 teaspoons vanilla extract (alcohol-free)
- 2 teaspoons orange flavor (alcohol-free)
- 2 tablespoons apricot or peach jam (sweetened with fruit juice)
- 3 ounces pineapple juice (sweetened with fruit juice)

Put the soy "cream cheese" into a medium sized mixing bowl. Stir with a spoon until somewhat creamy. Then, using an electric beater on low speed, beat the cream cheese until it is very creamy. Add the soy or rice milk and blend. Add the softened butter and blend well. Add the vanilla flavor, orange flavor, jam and juice. Beat on low speed until light and fluffy. Adjust the flavorings to your taste. Ice the cake and keep it refrigerated until serving.

Apple Cookies

Filling

- 2 medium sweet apples, peeled, cored and finely chopped
- 1 teaspoon cinnamon
- 1 teaspoon vanilla extract
- 1 tablespoon unsweetened applesauce
- 1 tablespoon unsweetened apple butter
- 1 tablespoon peach or apricot jam (sweetened with fruit juice)
- 2 tablespoons water
- pinch of nutmeg

Dough

- ¾ cup plus 1 tablespoon oat flour
- ¼ cup plus 1 tablespoon barley flour
- ½ teaspoon sea salt
- ½ teaspoon baking soda
- ¾ stick sweet butter, softened
- ¾ cup unsweetened applesauce
- ¼ cup unsweetened apple butter
- 4 tablespoons apricot or peach jam (sweetened with fruit juice)
- 1 egg
- 1 teaspoon vanilla extract

Lightly grease one or two cookie pans with some sweet butter. To make the filling, preheat oven to 350°. Put the chopped apples, 1 teaspoon cinnamon, 1 teaspoon vanilla extract, 1 tablespoon applesauce, 1 tablespoon apple butter, 1 tablespoon peach or apricot jam, 2 tablespoons of water and a pinch of nutmeg into a small baking dish. Stir the ingredients and bake 15-20 minutes until soft. Remove from oven and set aside. To make the dough, put the oat flour, barley flour, sea salt and baking soda into a sifter. Because oat flour tends to be lumpy, sift the ingredients twice and set aside. Using an electric mixer on low speed, cream the butter. Add the applesauce, apple butter and jam and beat until blended. Add the egg and vanilla extract and mix. The batter may not be completely blended like it would if you were using sugar, but do not be concerned. Add the flour mixture to the butter mixture and mix well. Add the apple mixture and stir. Cover the dough and put it into the refrigerator to chill for about 20-30 minutes. Turn the oven up to 375°. Drop a small amount of the batter from the tip of a teaspoon well apart. Bake about 10-12 minutes or until edges are lightly browned. Makes about 45 small cookies.

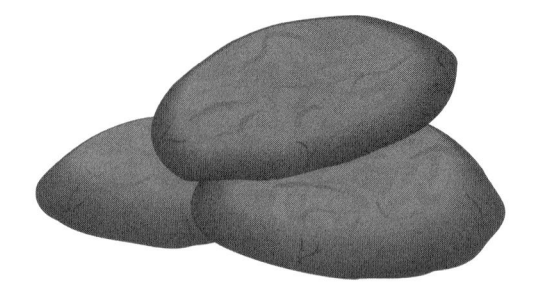

Barley Rice Cookies

- 1 cup barley flour
- 1 cup brown rice flour
- ½ teaspoon baking powder
- ½ teaspoon baking soda
- ½ teaspoon sea salt
- 1 teaspoon cinnamon
- 1 stick sweet butter, softened
- ¾ cup unsweetened applesauce
- ¼ cup unsweetened apple butter
- 1 egg, lightly beaten
- 1½ teaspoons vanilla extract
- 1 tablespoon vanilla or plain soy or rice milk
- 3 tablespoons apricot or peach jam (sweetened with fruit juice)
- Red raspberry, apricot or peach jam (sweetened with fruit juice) for the top of each cookie (optional, but good!)

Lightly grease one or two cookie pans with sweet butter. Sift the barley flour, brown rice flour, baking powder, baking soda, sea salt and cinnamon. Set the dry ingredients aside. In a large bowl, using an electric beater on low speed, cream the butter. Add the applesauce and apple butter and beat. Add the egg, vanilla extract, soy or rice milk and jam and blend. The batter may not be completely blended like it would if you were using sugar, but do not be concerned. Add the dry ingredients to the butter mixture and beat until well blended. Cover the dough and refrigerate it for about 20 minutes. Preheat the oven to 350°. You can either spread the batter over the entire cookie pan and cut into bars after baking or place round teaspoons of dough onto the pan about 2 inches apart. Put a little bit of red raspberry, apricot or peach jam on the top of each cookie, or if you are making bars, spread a thin coat of jam over the entire batter. Bake 15-20 minutes or until edges are lightly browned.

Carob Chip Cookies

This recipe is a wonderful substitute for regular chocolate chip cookies.

- ¾ cup plus 1 tablespoon oat flour
- ¼ cup plus 1 tablespoon barley flour
- ½ teaspoon sea salt
- ½ teaspoon baking soda
- ¾ stick sweet butter, softened
- ¾ cup unsweetened applesauce
- ¼ cup unsweetened apple butter
- 4 tablespoons apricot or peach jam (sweetened with fruit juice)
- 1 egg
- 1 teaspoon vanilla extract
- ½ cup unsweetened, dairy-free carob chips
- ½ cup unsweetened coconut (optional)

Lightly grease one or two cookie pans with sweet butter. Put the oat flour, barley flour, sea salt and baking soda into a sifter. Because oat flour tends to be lumpy, sift the ingredients twice and set aside. Using an electric mixer on low speed, cream the butter. Add the applesauce, apple butter and jam and beat until blended. Add the egg and vanilla extract and mix. The batter may not be completely blended like it would if you were using sugar, but do not be concerned. Add the flour mixture to the butter mixture and mix well. Stir in the carob chips. If using coconut, add it to the mixture and stir. Cover the dough and put it into the refrigerator to chill for about 20-30 minutes.

Cont'd

Carob Chip Cookies

Preheat the oven to 375°. Drop a small amount of the batter from the tip of a teaspoon — well apart. Bake about 15-18 minutes or until edges are lightly browned. Makes about 45 small cookies. You can replace the carob chips with a ½ cup of sifted carob flour to create a "chocolate cookie." Add the ½ cup of flour slowly until you have the flavor you desire. You can add the coconut if you like. Instead of using carob and coconut, put a little bit of your favorite jam (sweetened with fruit juice) on top of each cookie before baking. This basic dough is very good, so use it with any other ingredients that you like. There are endless possibilities!

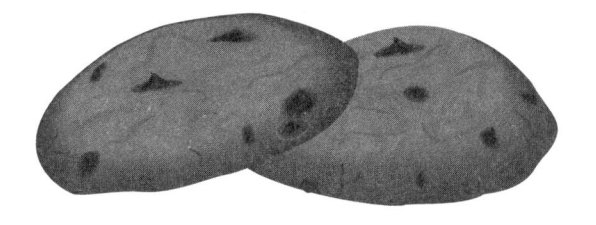

Oatmeal Cookies

- ¾ cup oat flour
- ¼ cup oat bran
- ½ teaspoon baking soda
- ½ teaspoon baking powder
- ½ teaspoon sea salt
- 1 teaspoon cinnamon
- ¾ stick sweet butter, softened
- ¾ cup unsweetened applesauce
- ¼ cup unsweetened apple butter
- 1 egg, lightly beaten
- 1½ teaspoons vanilla extract
- 1 tablespoon vanilla or plain soy or rice milk
- 3 tablespoons apricot or peach jam (sweetened with fruit juice)
- 1 cup uncooked oatmeal

Red raspberry, apricot or peach jam (sweetened with fruit juice) - for the top of each cookie

sweet butter

Sift the oat flour, oat bran, baking soda, baking powder, sea salt and cinnamon into a small bowl. Because oat flour tends to be lumpy, put the mixture back into the sifter and sift again. Set aside.

In a large bowl, using an electric beater on low speed, cream the butter. Add the applesauce and apple butter and beat. Add the egg, vanilla extract, soy or rice milk and 3 tablespoons of the apricot or peach jam and mix. The batter will not be completely blended like it would if you were using sugar, but do not be concerned. Add the dry ingredients to the butter mixture and beat. Add the uncooked oatmeal and beat well to combine. Cover the bowl and refrigerate the dough for about 20 minutes. Preheat the oven to 350°. Lightly grease one or two cookie pans with sweet butter. Place round teaspoons of dough onto the pan about 2 inches apart. Put a little dab of red raspberry, apricot or peach jam on the top of each cookie. Bake 15-20 minutes or until edges are lightly browned. Makes about two dozen cookies.

Apple Pancake

This makes a delicious Sunday morning breakfast or a wonderful dessert.

Filling

- 1 pound sweet apples (about 3-4 apples), peeled and thinly sliced
- 1 tablespoon sweet butter, melted
- 3 tablespoons apricot or peach jam (sweetened with fruit juice)
- 2 tablespoons unsweetened apple butter
- 1 teaspoon vanilla extract
- 1 teaspoon cinnamon
- pinch of nutmeg
- ¼ - ½ cup water

Pancake

- 2 tablespoons sweet butter
- 3 large eggs
- ¾ cup plain or vanilla soy or rice milk
- ¾ cup oat flour (sifted)
- ½ teaspoon sea salt

To make the filling, preheat oven to 350°. Put the melted butter, jam, apple butter, vanilla, cinnamon, nutmeg and water into a baking dish. Mix the ingredients until well blended. Add the thinly sliced apples and mix gently until coated. Bake 30-40 minutes or until the apples are soft, stirring occasionally. Take the apples out of the oven. Keep fruit warm until ready to serve.

Cont'd

Apple Pancake

To make the pancake, turn the oven up to 450°. Melt butter in a 10½ x 15 baking dish and coat the dish. Using a whisk, beat eggs, soy or rice milk, oat flour and sea salt until smooth. Pour the batter into the dish and place it in the oven. Bake for 10 minutes and then lower oven to 350° and bake another 10 minutes or until nicely browned. If pancake bubbles, pierce with a fork. Remove the pancake from the oven and put the apple mixture on top of the pancake. Fold sides of pancake over to cover the apples. Rub a little bit of butter on top of the pancake (optional) and serve immediately.

Pie Crust

1   cup spelt, oat, brown rice or any flour in your food plan

3   tablespoons cold water
4   tablespoons cold canola oil

Preheat oven to 350°. Put all ingredients into a mixing bowl. Stir with a spoon until the dough is well mixed. Put the dough into a pie plate and using your fingers, press the dough evenly around the plate. Bake for 20 minutes and remove from the oven. Put your favorite pie filling into the pre-baked pie crust and continue baking according to your recipe's instructions. I find the spelt flour to be the most flavorful, but try the different flours to see which one you like best.

Crumb Topping

½   cup flour (use the same flour in this recipe that you are using for your pie crust)
1   teaspoon cinnamon

1   tablespoon water
1   tablespoon canola oil
pinch of sea salt
sweet butter

Put all the ingredients into a mixing bowl. Mix ingredients with a spoon until crumbly. Sprinkle on top of pie and dot with a few small pieces of sweet butter. Bake according to your recipe's instructions.

Apple Pie

Make a pie crust according to the directions on page 101.

Filling

- 2 lbs. sweet apples
- 1 teaspoon cinnamon
- ⅛ teaspoon nutmeg
- ⅛ teaspoon sea salt
- 2 tablespoons spelt or oat flour (same as pie crust)
- ½ teaspoon or more of vanilla extract
- ½ bag of frozen blueberries, cherries or strawberries (optional)
- 1 cup unsweetened applesauce
- 3 tablespoons unsweetened apple butter
- 2-3 tablespoons peach or apricot jam (sweetened with fruit juice)

Preheat oven to 300°. Peel and slice apples. Mix cinnamon, nutmeg, sea salt and flour in a small bowl and set aside. In a large bowl, mix vanilla, berries, applesauce, apple butter and jam. Put apples into the bowl with the wet ingredients and mix carefully. Add the dry ingredients and mix. Put into 9 inch pre-baked pie crust and dot with a little butter if you like. Bake for 1 hour or until apples are soft.

You can substitute ripe peaches for apples. Place fresh peaches into boiling water for a few minutes and remove to a bowl. Peel the skin off the peaches, slice and mix with peach and apricot jam, ½ cup of applesauce and dry ingredients. You can use blueberries with peaches as well. If you want to have more liquid in the pie, add ¼ - ½ cup of plain or vanilla soy or rice milk to the wet ingredients.

Banana Custard Pie

Make a pie crust and crumb topping (page 101) This pie can be made without a pie crust, but be sure to lightly grease the pie plate with sweet butter before filling with the mixture.

Filling

- 4 ripe bananas, mashed
- 2 ripe bananas, sliced
- 1 cup vanilla soy or rice milk
- 1 egg
- 2 teaspoons vanilla extract
- 1/8 teaspoon orange flavor (no alcohol)
- 2 tablespoons apricot or peach jam (sweetened with fruit juice)
- 1/2 teaspoon cinnamon
- 1/8 teaspoon sea salt
- 1 tablespoon arrowroot mixed with 2 ounces of vanilla soy or rice milk

sweet butter

Preheat oven to 350°. Put mashed bananas, vanilla soy or rice milk, egg, vanilla extract, orange flavor, jam, cinnamon, sea salt and arrowroot mixture into a food processor and blend well - about 1 minute. Pour mixture into a pre-baked pie crust or lightly greased pie plate and bake for 20 minutes. Remove pie from oven and cover entire surface of pie with the sliced bananas. Sprinkle the crumb topping over the sliced bananas. Dot with sweet butter and bake another 20 minutes.

Bread Pudding

- 8-10 slices oat flour bread, broken up (see oat flour bread recipe page 82)
- 2 tablespoons melted butter
- 1 teaspoon cinnamon
- 1 teaspoon vanilla extract
- 2 cups soy milk (plain or vanilla)
- 4 eggs
- ½ bag unsweetened blueberries (leave whole)
- ½ bag unsweetened strawberries, defrosted and mashed
- ½ cup unsweetened applesauce
- ¼ cup unsweetened apple butter

Preheat oven to 350°. Grease a 1½ quart baking dish with some sweet butter. Put broken pieces of bread in baking dish. Sprinkle cinnamon and pour the melted butter over the bread. In a separate bowl, beat eggs, stir in soy milk and vanilla and pour over bread. Add fruit, applesauce and apple butter and stir. Set pan in another pan that has 1 inch of hot water in it. Bake about 40 minutes. Serve warm or chilled. Rice bread and rice milk may be substituted for the oat bread and soy milk.

Baked Apple

1 apple (cut a diamond shape out of the top of the apple)

cinnamon
vanilla extract
water

Preheat oven to 350°. Put apple into a shallow baking dish. Add about ½ cup of water. Sprinkle cinnamon and put a little vanilla into the hole in the top of the apple. Put the small piece back into its place on the top of the apple. Bake for about 40 minutes or until soft.

Banana Custard

Peel a very ripe banana. Chop it, put it into a freezer bag and freeze it overnight. Take the banana out and put it into a food processor. It will be like pudding.

Index

APPETIZERS 14
   Black Bean Hummus 14
   Lentil Paté 15
   Onion Dip 16
   Tofu Dip 17
BREADS & PANCAKES 82
   Barley Biscuits 85
   Barley Pancakes 87
   Homemade Wheat-Free Bread Crumbs 88
   Homemade Chips 88
   Oat Biscuits 85
   Oat Flour Bread 82
   Oat Flour Pancakes 86
   Rice Baking Mix Bread 82
   Rice Baking Mix Muffins 84
   Rice Baking Mix Pancakes 86
   Rice Baking Mix Waffles 87
   Rice Waffles 87
   Spelt Muffins 83
DESSERTS 89
   Apple Cookies 93, 94
   Apple Pancake 99, 100
   Apple Pie 102
   Baked Apple 105
   Banana Cake or Apple Cake 90
   Banana Custard 105
   Banana Custard Pie 103
   Barley Rice Cookies 95
   Bread Pudding 104
   Carob Chip Cookies 96, 97
   Carrot Cake 91
   Crumb Topping 101
   Oatmeal Cookies 98
   Pie Crust 101

DESSERTS cont'd: 89
    Soy "Cream Cheese" Icing 92
    Sweet Potato Pudding 41, 42
DRIED BEANS & LENTILS 72
    Aurora's Spanish Black Beans 79
    Aurora's Spanish Kidney Beans 80
    "Baked Beans" 73
    Black Beans 74
    Chickpea Pancakes 75
    Gertie's Chili 76
    Lentil Loaf 77
    Refried Beans 78
EATING OUT 10
GRAINS 81
    White Basmati Rice 81
MISCELLANEOUS
    An Efficient Kitchen 1
    Perfect Snack 88
    Sample Menu 2
POULTRY 51
    Broccoli Quiche 58
    Chicken Breasts 51
    Chicken Fricassee 52
    Chicken Meatballs 53
    Chicken Pot Pie 54
    Ground Turkey 60
    Italian Meat Sauce 63
    Lasagne 64
    Madame A's Chicken in a Pan 55
    Madame A's Lemon Garlic Chicken 56
    Omelette in the Oven 57
    Spinach Quiche 59
    Turkey Chili 60
    Turkey Meat Loaf 61
    Turkey Meatballs and Italian Gravy 62

RECIPES 13
RECOMMENDED FOOD AND MISCELLANEOUS PRODUCTS 5
    Bread, Bread Products, Cookies, Cereal, Pasta 5
    Canned Foods 6
    Flour for Baking Bread Products 7
    Frozen Foods 7
    Grains 8
    Miscellaneous Food Products 8,9
    Miscellaneous Non-Food Products 9
SALAD DRESSINGS, SAUCES AND MARINADES 46
    Basic White Sauce 47
    Cathy's Marinara Sauce 47
    Lemon Oil Salad Dressing 46
    Marinade for Chicken, Fish, or Tofu 49
    Marinade for Chicken or Tofu 49
    Quick Salad Dressing 46
    Seafood Marinade 50
    Sweet and Sour Sauce for Chicken or Tofu 48
    White Sauce (3 variations) 48
SEAFOOD 65
    Baked Fish Fillets 65
    Baked Salmon 66
    Broiled, Baked or Grilled Salmon 66
    Scallops, Spinach, Mushrooms and Garlic 67
INGREDIENT SUBSTITUTES 11,12
SHOPPING GUIDE FOR FOOD AND MISCELLANEOUS PRODUCTS .. 3, 4
SOUPS 18
    Lentil Soup 18
    Minestrone 19
    Mushroom Barley Soup 20
    Myra's Chicken Soup 22
    Split Pea Soup 21
    Vegetable Bean Soup 23
    Vegetable Soup 24

TOFU 68
    Breakfast Tofu 68, 69
    Italian Tofu Stew 69
    Tofu Chili 70
    Tofu Spinach Pie 71
VEGETABLES 25
    Avocado Salad 28
    Broiled Broccoli with Garlic 31
    Butternut Squash Bake 45
    Denise's Potato Salad 36
    Eggplant Parmigiana 33
    Grandma Rose's Roasted Carrots 32
    Green Bean Casserole 29
    Grilled Vegetables 27
    Mashed Potatoes and Spinach 37
    Oven "Fried" Sweet Onions 35
    Oven Roasted Home "Fried" Potatoes 38
    Potato Pancakes 39
    Roasted Eggplant and Garbanzo Beans 34
    Roasted Root Vegetables 43
    Roasted Vegetables 26
    Sautéed Vegetables 27
    Sliced Sweet Potatoes 40
    Stir Fried Green Beans 30
    Stir Fry 26
    Summer Salad 44
    Sweet Potato Pudding 41, 42
    Sweet Potatoes 40

You can contact Janet Lasky

by writing to:

Janet Lasky
P.O. Box 713
Sparta, NJ 07871

or e-mail at:

janet@higher-choices.com

visit her web site at:

www.higher-choices.com

Order Form

If you would like to order more books, fill out the form below and return it with a personal check, postal or bank money order to: Higher Choices, P.O. Box 713, Sparta, New Jersey 07871.

Each book is $15.95 plus $3.00 for shipping the first book and $1.00 for shipping each additional book. Add 6% sales tax for books shipped to New Jersey addresses.

Name: _____

Address:_____

City:_____State:_____Zip:_____-_____

Telephone: _____

e-mail address:_____

Order Form For A Friend

If you would like to order more books, fill out the form below and return it with a personal check, postal or bank money order to: Higher Choices, P.O. Box 713, Sparta, New Jersey 07871.

Each book is $15.95 plus $3.00 for shipping the first book and $1.00 for shipping each additional book. Add 6% sales tax for books shipped to New Jersey addresses.

Name: _____

Address: _____

City: _____ State: _____ Zip: _____ - _____

Telephone: _____

e-mail address: _____